Great Writing 5

Greater Essays

Great Writing 5

Greater Essays

SECOND EDITION

KEITH S. FOLSE
UNIVERSITY OF CENTRAL FLORIDA

TISON PUGH
UNIVERSITY OF CENTRAL FLORIDA

HEINLE
CENGAGE Learning

Australia • Canada • Mexico • Singapore • Spain • United Kingdom • United States

HEINLE
CENGAGE Learning™

**Great Writing 5: Greater Essays,
Second Edition**
Keith S. Folse, Tison Pugh

Publisher: Sherrise Roehr

Acquisition Editor: Tom Jefferies

Senior Development Editor: Yeny Kim

Assistant Editor: Marissa Petrarca

Director of Content and Media Production:
Michael Burggren

Marketing Director, U.S.: Jim McDonough

Director of Adult Education Sales:
Eric Bredenberg

Marketing Communications Manager:
Beth Leonard

Senior Product Marketing Manager:
Katie Kelley

Academic Marketing Manager:
Caitlin Driscoll

Senior Content Project Manager:
Maryellen Eschmann-Killeen

Senior Print Buyer: Susan Spencer

Composition: Pre-Press PMG

Library of Congress Control Number: 2009932091

ISBN-13: 978-1-4240-6211-9

ISBN-10: 1-4240-6211-X

Heinle, Cengage Learning
20 Channel Center Street
Boston, MA 02210
USA

Cengage learning is a leading provider of customized learning solutions with
office locations around the globe, including Singapore, the United Kingdom,
Australia, Mexico, Brazil, and Japan. Locate our local office at: **International.
cengage.com/region**

Cengage Learning products are represented in Canada by Nelson Education, Ltd.

Visit Heinle online at **elt.heinle.com**
Visit out corporate website at **cengage.com**

Printed in the United States of America
2 3 4 5 6 7 13 12 11 10

Contents

w to the Second Edition

me important changes have been made to this second edition. The following new features have been
in this new edition and build on the existing strengths of *Great Writing 5* while providing additional
rt and supplemental material to equip students to succeed at building greater writing skills.

ling Better Sentences

each unit, students are asked to turn to Appendix 1 and work on building better sentences. This
y focuses on students' sentence-level writing skills using content from the essays. Individual
ces taken from the essays have been isolated and divided into short, choppy sentences that students
ked to combine into longer sentences. After completing the exercises, students are able to check their
n products with the original sentences found in the example essays. This short activity lends itself
small groups and can then be checked by the whole class, thus not generating papers that require
r correction.

d Writing

ne final activity in each unit features a timed-writing assignment. Students are given a writing prompt
idelines. Students are then asked to complete the writing task within a certain amount of time.

though we have placed the Timed Writing as a final task within each unit, some teachers may prefer
gn this topic as the first task of the unit. Using this method, teachers can collect students' work and
ave them rewrite their essays at the end of the unit. In this way, students enjoy two opportunities to
e composition while teachers only read and mark papers once.

ions and Plagiarism

ne Citations and Plagiarism section of the Handbook is new to this second edition, but the topic
esses is not a new concern: how to cite borrowed information and to avoid plagiarism. For many
ts, the notion of plagiarism is new. Many English learners find it difficult to paraphrase material
e they either do not understand the original material well enough or they do not have enough
lary knowledge to express the same idea in their own words. Whether writers use a paraphrase or
ct quotation, they need to learn how to cite this information to avoid plagiarism.

ching from This Book

ere are as many ways to use *Great Writing 5* as there are composition teachers. We hope that the
ng material and the array of activities, tasks, and checklists will serve as a solid guide to help students
te the process of writing paragraphs and essays.

en the best of writers will struggle through the process in the never-ending task of phrasing their
its in the most clear and appropriate manner. For students, these challenges can be daunting.
Writing 5 seeks to alleviate much of the stress of writing through a series of exercises and writing
unities, but we rely on the teachers in the classrooms to help their students achieve their potential
ers. To that end, *Great Writing 5* is a helpful tool, one that we hope you will find useful as you bring
e best from your students.

For the answer key, additional exercises, and other instructor resources, visit the *Great Writing 5*
instructor Web site: elt.heinle.com/greatwriting
Additional exercises for each unit are available to students on the *Great Writing 5* student Web site:
elt.heinle.com/greatwriting

Overview

Great Writing 5: Greater Essays gives students opportunities to develop thei
well as their overall language skills. The heart of this book lies in the concept th
to become better writers by learning to become better editors of their own essa
essays. Just as professional writers have editors to help them hone their prose, s
helpful guidance throughout the writing process—from brainstorming, outlini
final product.

To this end, *Great Writing 5* models the revision process for students, dem
unit an essay's first draft, the same draft with teacher's comments, and a final d
has revised in response to the teacher's suggestions. Many writing books addre
peer review, but *Great Writing 5* incorporates the revising process into a mana
pedagogical practice. Time is spent on individual writing, but time is also dedi
in groups to revise short compositions or to combine pieces of information int
constructed sentences.

Because we hope to help students learn through more engaged revision in *G*
emphasize the importance of having a varied vocabulary for effective essay writi
high-level vocabulary is essential for effective communication. Numerous studie
low level of vocabulary skills among writing students. *Great Writing 5* tackles thi
directly through a series of exercises addressing vocabulary, including not only t
definition practice but also collocation practice so that students become familiar
vocabulary items in an academic context.

Three distinguishing features of this book are (1) the multiple drafts of each e
essay, the same essay with teacher's comments, and the student's revised draft bas
comments), (2) the connected vocabulary activities (including collocation practi
focused grammar points per unit with supporting exercises.

Great Writing 5 contains a wealth of materials for the classroom. The new sec
activities, including six sample essays with multiple drafts and 60 suggestions for
assignments.

Text Organization

In the first unit of *Great Writing 5*, we provide a general overview of essays. I
units, we discuss in detail five types of essays: process analysis, comparison, caus
and narrative. (These five types may be covered in any order, based on the teache
learning goals.) For each type of essay, we discuss its particular objectives and rh
well as provide practice activities in prewriting, revising, organizing, writing effe
improving grammar skills. The book ends with a Brief Writer's Handbook with A
supplemental instruction and practice with sentence construction, grammar, wo
section that addresses citations and plagiarism. The Handbook is followed by tw
Building Better Sentences section and Peer Editing Sheets.

add
sup

Bu

acti
sen
are
wri
wel
teac

Tin

and

to a
ther
prac

Cit

it ad
stud
beca
voca
an e

Te

teac
navi

thou
Grea
oppo
as le
forth

Acknowledgments

We would like to thank our composition colleagues who generously shared their ideas, insights, and feedback on writing, community college and university English course requirements, and textbook design. Because of their input, this book reflects the needs of real teachers in real classrooms.

We offer special thanks to our incredible editors. Very special kudos go to our developmental editors Yeny Kim and Marissa Petrarca, who have worked so diligently to make this second edition of *Great Writing 5* come to fruition. We remain indebted to our first acquisitions editor Susan Maguire, our first editor Kathy Sands Boehmer, and our first development editor Kathleen Smith. Without all the help and input of these people, this book would not be the tremendous asset that it has become.

We would also like to thank the following reviewers who offered ideas and suggestions that shaped our revisions:

Andrew Barnette, University of Mississippi, MS
Leslie Biaggi, Miami Dade College, FL
Marta Dmytrenko-Ahrabian, Wayne State University, MI
Nicholas Hilmers, DePaul University, IL
Marta Menendez, Miami Dade College, FL
Alan Shute, Bunker Hill Community College, MA
Wendy Whitacre, University of Arizona, AZ

Finally, many thanks go to our students, who have taught us what composition ought to be. Without them, this work would have no purpose.

Keith S. Folse
Tison Pugh

Guided Tour

✳ NEW TO THIS EDITION

A new **four-color design** allows for engaging, easy-to-follow lessons.

Cause-Effect Essays | Unit 4

GOAL: To learn how to write a cause-effect essay

*Grammar Topics: 4.1 Maintaining consistent pronouns; 4.2 Sentence fragments;
4.3 Consistent verb tense; 4.4 Confusing words: *it's / its*; 4.5 Word parts

What Is a Cause-Effect Essay?

We all understand cause-effect relationships. For example, if you stay up late the night before a test, hanging out with friends and not studying, you will likely not perform well on the test. A **cause-effect essay** tells how one event (the cause) leads to another event (the effect).

Typically, cause-effect essays work in one of two ways:

- They analyze the ways in which several effects result from a particular cause. ("Focus-on-Effects" Method)
- They analyze the ways in which several causes lead to a particular effect. ("Focus-on-Causes" Method)

Either approach is an effective means of discussing the possible relationship between the two events.

In cause-effect essays, it is easy to suggest that because one event preceded another event, the former event caused the latter. Simply because one event follows another event sequentially does not mean that the two actions are related. For example, people often complain that as soon as they finish washing their car, it starts to rain. Obviously, washing a car does not cause rain. Writers need to be sure that the cause-effect relationship they describe is logical.

Writing Goals at the beginning of every unit provide a clear road map for the instruction that follows.

Writing models help students focus on specific writing skills and multiple rhetorical structures.

ACTIVITY 4 First Draft of the Essay

As you read this first draft, look for areas that need improvement.

ESSAY 4A

Music, Computers, and the Recording Industry

The recording industry is in a big hole. Albums and CDs are not selling as much as several years ago, and this **trend** shows no sign of reversing. For the industry as a whole, profits are down ten percent inside the last three year. What has caused this downward **spiral** for the music industry? The answer is an equipment with which I am writing this essay: the personal computer. There are three reasons that the computer has had a bad effect in the recording industry.

Due to it is popular to share computer sound files, consumers no longer feel that they are need to purchase music. Many people think it is **morally** acceptable—not to mention convenience—to download music files for free via file-sharing services. A couple of mouse-button click, and **presto**! Now you "own" on your own computer that nice little tune that you have been **humming.** Then it was just a couple of more clicks until it was burned on a CD for you. With this level of convenience, it was easy to see why record companies are **feeling the pinch.**

Computers allow music people to **market** and sell their own music. Music people can record and create their own CDs at a relatively **modest** cost these days. Before the development of the personal computer, this would have been impossible. For this reason, it makes less sense for music people to give away a part of their profits to a record company for activities that he can accomplish themselves.

The recording industry bears some of the blame for its own problems. Simply because they have been shy about using personal computers to sell its products. It has long annoy me that record companies primarily sell albums when all I want is one song. Too many albums

contained only one good song, and I do not like to spend money for an entire album when I wanted only one song. The recording industry should package and sell music in a way that consumers want. And take advantage of personal computers to market songs to individual consumers.

If the downward trends in the recording industry continues, there will still be a recording industry? It is quite possible that the recording industry will stop over time if it becomes no longer profitable for them to market and sell music. Performing artists have to advertise themselves through smaller **venues**, and consumers might need to seek out new music if its no longer marketed directly to us. The computer will **bring about** tremendous changes to the recording industry. The industry will have to move quickly to **retain** its **relevance** in the today's economy.

---

a trend: a new style that people follow
a spiral: a winding curve that moves toward a fixed center
morally: ethically, honorably
presto: an expression that indicates something has been accomplished instantly
hum: to sing without words
feel the pinch: to suffer the consequences

market: to sell or offer something for sale
modest: moderate in amount
a venue: a location
bring about: to cause to happen
retain: to keep possession of something
relevance: importance in relation to the matter being considered

ACTIVITY 7 Analyzing the Content

Answer these questions about the revised version (Essay 4C) of "Modern Music Technology: Downloading or Stealing?"

1. What is the topic? _____

2. Write the thesis statement here: _____
   _____

3. What is the effect that the writer describes in the essay?
   _____
   _____
   _____

4. What are some of the causes that the writer describes?
   _____
   _____
   _____

5. Is the writer's reasoning convincing? _____
   How could it be improved? _____
   _____

ACTIVITY 8 Analyzing the Organization

Read the outline of "Modern Music Technology: Downloading or Stealing?" Then use information in the box to complete the outline.

- a decrease in sales of CDs and albums
- current conditions
- the recording industry
- personal computer
- musicians

I. Introduction
   A. Describe the current troubled situation of the recording industry.
   B. Thesis statement: The _____ has caused many
      of the recording industry's woes.

Guided, structured activities help students to quickly master writing tasks.

II. Body Paragraph 1: Show that the popularity of sharing computer files has led to _____
    _____

III. Body Paragraph 2: Describe how computers allow _____
     to market their own music without the recording industry.

IV. Body Paragraph 3: Suggest that _____ bears some
    responsibility because it has not marketed through personal computers.

V. Conclusion
   A. Ponder the future of the recording industry if _____ remain.
   B. Suggest that the recording industry must act quickly to reverse these declines.

Writer's Note

Language for Conversation and for Writing

   Language in conversation, especially between people who know each other well, is usually informal. Language in writing, in contrast, is often more formal. Language in writing has a different style than language in conversation. We use different vocabulary and sometimes different structures for conversation and for writing.

   Here are some examples of differences in these two language styles.

Conversation	Writing
kids	children
a cool movie	a great movie, a really interesting movie
See you later!	I hope to see you soon.
Well, this is the reason . . .	The reason is . . .

Can you think of other pairs that are more appropriate for conversation or for writing?

Building Better Sentences

   Correct and varied sentence structure is essential to the quality of your writing. For further practice with "Modern Music Technology: Downloading or Stealing?" go to Practice 4 on page 205 in Appendix 1.

Writer's Note sections provide relevant writing-skill instruction that supports the unit's writing goals.

NEW TO THIS EDITION

Building Better Sentences boxes help students improve sentence-level writing skills using content from the essays.

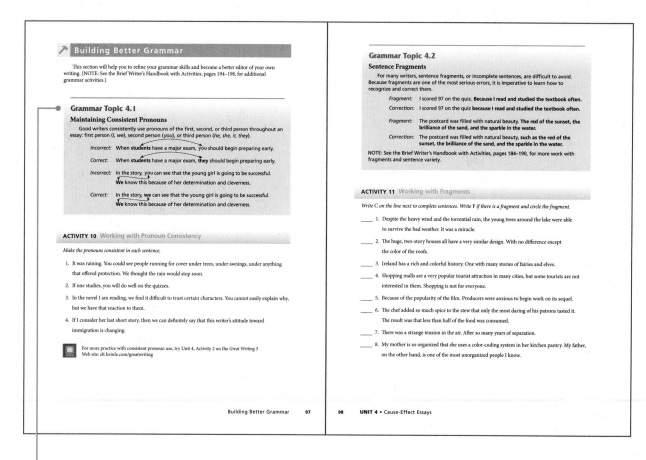

Building Better Grammar

This section will help you to refine your grammar skills and become a better editor of your own writing. (NOTE: See the Brief Writer's Handbook with Activities, pages 194–198, for additional grammar activities.)

Grammar Topic 4.1
Maintaining Consistent Pronouns

Good writers consistently use pronouns of the first, second, or third person throughout an essay: first person (*I, we*), second person (*you*), or third person (*he, she, it, they*).

Incorrect: When **students** have a major exam, **you** should begin preparing early.

Correct: When **students** have a major exam, **they** should begin preparing early.

Incorrect: In the story, **you** can see that the young girl is going to be successful. **We** know this because of her determination and cleverness.

Correct: In the story, **we** can see that the young girl is going to be successful. **We** know this because of her determination and cleverness.

ACTIVITY 10 Working with Pronoun Consistency

Make the pronouns consistent in each sentence.

1. It was raining. You could see people running for cover under trees, under awnings, under anything that offered protection. We thought the rain would stop soon.

2. If one studies, you will do well on the quizzes.

3. In the novel I am reading, we find it difficult to trust certain characters. You cannot easily explain why, but we have that reaction to them.

4. If I consider her last short story, then we can definitely say that this writer's attitude toward immigration is changing.

For more practice with consistent pronoun use, try Unit 4, Activity 2 on the *Great Writing 5* Web site: elt.heinle.com/greatwriting

Building Better Grammar   97

---

98   UNIT 4 • Cause-Effect Essays

Grammar Topic 4.2
Sentence Fragments

For many writers, sentence fragments, or incomplete sentences, are difficult to avoid. Because fragments are one of the most serious errors, it is imperative to learn how to recognize and correct them.

Fragment: I scored 97 on the quiz. **Because I read and studied the textbook often.**

Correction: I scored 97 on the quiz **because I read and studied the textbook often.**

Fragment: The postcard was filled with natural beauty. **The red of the sunset, the brilliance of the sand, and the sparkle in the water.**

Correction: The postcard was filled with natural beauty, **such as the red of the sunset, the brilliance of the sand, and the sparkle in the water.**

NOTE: See the Brief Writer's Handbook with Activities, pages 184–190, for more work with fragments and sentence variety.

ACTIVITY 11 Working with Fragments

Write C on the line next to complete sentences. Write F if there is a fragment and circle the fragment.

_____ 1. Despite the heavy wind and the torrential rain, the young trees around the lake were able to survive the bad weather. It was a miracle.

_____ 2. The huge, two-story houses all have a very similar design. With no difference except the color of the roofs.

_____ 3. Ireland has a rich and colorful history. One with many stories of fairies and elves.

_____ 4. Shopping malls are a very popular tourist attraction in many cities, but some tourists are not interested in them. Shopping is not for everyone.

_____ 5. Because of the popularity of the film. Producers were anxious to begin work on its sequel.

_____ 6. The chef added so much spice to the stew that only the most daring of his patrons tasted it. The result was that less than half of the food was consumed.

_____ 7. There was a strange tension in the air. After so many years of separation.

_____ 8. My mother is so organized that she uses a color-coding system in her kitchen pantry. My father, on the other hand, is one of the most unorganized people I know.

Integrated **grammar** lessons teach and practice the grammar necessary to accomplish the writing goals of the unit.

_____ 7. Simon argued that the judge was incompetent in the trial and that a mistrial should be declared.

_____ 8. The car needs a new paint job since it's trunk is getting rusty.

_____ 9. Akio knew the truth, but she was afraid to tell the police.

_____ 10. Due to the large influx of immigrants into Canada beginning in the 1950s.

For more practice with the grammar topics from this unit, try Unit 4, Activity 4 on the *Great Writing 5* Web site: elt.heinle.com/greatwriting

ACTIVITY 16 Editing a Paragraph: Review of Grammar Topics 4.1–4.5

Seven of the ten underlined portions in the following paragraph contain an error involving one of the grammar topics featured in this unit. Correct the errors on the lines provided. If the word or phrase is correct, write C.

EXAMPLE PARAGRAPH

The Impact of E-mail on Communication

(1.) <u>On</u> _____ e-mail, messages are composed, transmitted, and usually read on computer (2.) <u>screens. Today</u> _____ e-mail has replaced the (3.) <u>telephone. As</u> _____ the preferred medium to communicate in business. In 1997, for the first time ever, more e-mail was sent than letters via the post office. In a recent American Management Association (4.) <u>surveying,</u> _____ 36 percent of executives reported that (5.) <u>you</u> _____ favor e-mail for most management (6.) <u>communicate,</u> _____ compared with 26 percent who preferred the phone. Surprisingly, one of the less (7.) <u>popular</u> _____ alternatives was a face-to-face meeting, favored by only 15 percent of the (8.) <u>executives. One</u> _____ executive said, "(9.) <u>Its</u> _____ only a matter of time before we do away with face-to-face business deals (10.) <u>complete</u> _____."

102   UNIT 4 • Cause-Effect Essays

Individual and peer **editing** opportunities in every unit provide focused guidelines for effective editing practice.

xvi

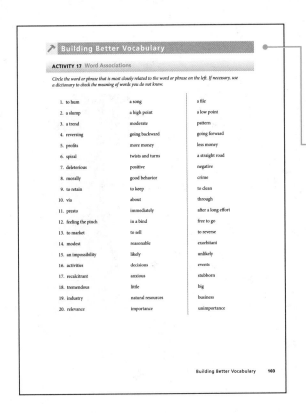

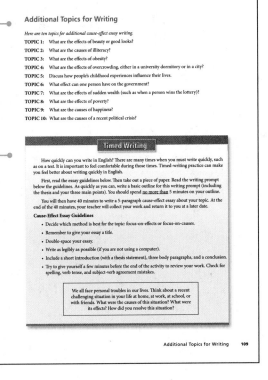

NEW TO THIS EDITION

Building Better Vocabulary features teach students how to accurately and effectively use written English.

Additional Topics for Writing activities in each unit provide the opportunity for more expressive, opinion-driven pieces of writing.

NEW TO THIS EDITION

Timed writing activities prepare students for success on standardized tests like the TOEFL®.

Supplements

NEW TO THIS EDITION

The **Assessment CD-ROM with** *ExamView®* allows teachers to create tests and quizzes easily.

NEW TO THIS EDITION

The **Classroom Presentation Tool** makes instruction clearer and learning simpler.

For **Instructor's Resources** like lesson-planning tips, please visit elt.heinle.com/greatwriting.

An Introduction to Writing Essays

Unit 1

GOAL: To learn about the structure of a five-paragraph essay

*Grammar Topics: **1.1** Nouns and verbs; **1.2** Adjectives; **1.3** Prepositions; **1.4** Confusing words: articles *a/an*; **1.5** Word forms

What Is an Essay?

ESSAY	a short written composition on one topic that expresses the views of the writer

What would the world be like if there were no words? Consider how often we think, speak, read, and communicate with words. How would we talk to our family and friends, or how would we fulfill our basic needs for food, shelter, and clothing if we did not have access to language?

We are surrounded every day by the written word, as seen in notes, letters, instruction manuals, books, e-mails, Web sites, magazines, and essays. What are essays? **Essays** are short written compositions that share our thoughts about a given topic with an audience. Whether that audience is a teacher, fellow students, or the world beyond the classroom, an essay expresses the writer's point of view so that it may be fully understood. In this book, we will study how we communicate our ideas effectively through essays.

How Is an Essay Organized?

Though essays vary greatly in their subject matter and style of writing, the most common academic essays share a similar structure. They are usually made up of at least five paragraphs organized in three basic parts: an **introduction**, a **body**, and a **conclusion**.

INTRODUCTION	Paragraph 1
BODY	Paragraphs 2, 3, 4
CONCLUSION	Paragraph 5

Some common types of academic essays, all of which you will study in this book, include **process analysis, comparison, cause-effect, argumentative,** and **narrative** essays. Many essays are actually a combination of different kinds of essays. For example, an essay may compare two potential plans, discuss the effects of each, and then attempt to persuade you that one plan is better than the other. If you learn how to write these different kinds of essays, you will also be able to write a mixed essay effectively.

✎ Writer's Note

The Five-Paragraph Essay

The most common form of essay that is taught in textbooks is the five-paragraph essay. In a typical five-paragraph essay, paragraph 1 introduces the topic, paragraphs 2-4 develop the topic by giving details, and paragraph 5 concludes the essay. The five-paragraph essay form is emphasized because it allows writers great freedom to explain their ideas on a given topic to their readers. At the same time, the traditional assignment in many writing classes is a five-paragraph essay. In addition, if you understand how to write a five-paragraph essay, you can easily expand this structure to include more paragraphs to address increasingly complex and sophisticated ideas. An essay can range from three paragraphs to ten or more. Regardless of the length of your essay, it should always consist of an introduction, a body, and a conclusion.

ACTIVITY 1 Reading an Example Essay

Read the following essay. Can you identify which paragraphs are the introduction, the body, and the conclusion?

EXAMPLE ESSAY

Against E-Voting

1   Have you ever considered the argument that computers threaten democracy? With computer technology advancing daily, we know that many activities that used to take many long hours can now be **accomplished** in a few minutes, or even seconds. For the most part, these technological **innovations** promise to save us time and money and to make our lives easier and more comfortable. Despite the greater efficiency of computers in so many areas, we should not turn over all aspects of our lives to computers. In particular, I believe that we should not vote with computers or other electronic media because democracy is too important to **cede** to the unreliability of cyberspace.

accomplished: completed
an innovation: a new idea or system

cede: to yield

2   In years past, people voted on paper ballots and marked them with ink or some similar means. Voters could see the choices they made. They could look back over their ballot to ensure that they did not make a mistake. Also, if arguments **arose** over the outcome of an election, paper ballots allowed election officials to count votes by hand. This process may be **tedious,** but it has the benefit of being **verifiable.** Several countries still use this traditional method of voting, and it provides a crucial foundation for ensuring fairness.

3   If this traditional system of voting is not used, however, voters do not really know whether their votes are **tallied** accurately with e-voting systems. It is quite possible that a computer technician could develop a program so that a person could select one candidate on a computer screen, yet the vote would be counted for another candidate. Although some people might think this scenario sounds **paranoid**, consider how many stories you hear in the news about **breaches** in computer security. The simple fact is that **hackers** can gain access to many computer systems for illegal purposes. By illegally entering into a cyber-**polling** station, they could easily change the outcome of an election.

4   If voting commissions decide to use electronic voting machines in their districts, they would be well advised to ensure that all voters receive receipts for their votes that would then be collected for subsequent verification. In this manner, voters could make sure that their receipts stated clearly that they did in fact vote for the candidates they desired. Furthermore, if any candidate suspected that the election was unfair, these receipts could be counted by hand and checked against the results that the computers provided.

5   Computer technologies have improved the qualities of our lives vastly, but these technologies are not a **panacea** for all of society's troubles. Sometimes, a little more human work ensures a better result. Since voting is critically important to the effective and honest working of democracies, we should rely on a much older technology—paper and ink—rather than on computers for all of our elections.

arise: to come into being, appear
tedious: tiresome, boring
verifiable: able to be proven true or accurate
tallied: counted, listed, recorded
paranoid: irrationally suspicious

a breach: a hole or break in a security system
a hacker: a person who gains access to computer systems to steal information or money
polling: voting
a panacea: a cure for all diseases or problems

Building Better Sentences

Correct and varied sentence structure is essential to the quality of your writing. For further practice with "Against E-Voting," go to Practice 1 on page 203 in Appendix 1.

How Do You Write an Introduction?

INTRODUCTION	1. gives background information
	2. presents the topic—that is, the primary subject of the essay
	3. includes a thesis statement—the writer's ideas about or position on the topic

The first paragraph of a five-paragraph essay is the **introduction.** The introduction has three objectives.
  1. It gives background information to connect the reader to the topic.
  2. It presents the topic, which is the subject of the essay.
  3. The thesis statement summarizes the main point of the essay and explains the writer's idea or position about the topic. In short, the thesis statement gives the writer's plan for the essay.

What Is the Difference between the Topic and the Thesis Statement?

The **topic** is the general subject of the essay. The **thesis statement,** on the other hand, is a specific sentence that explains the writer's position about the topic.

TOPIC	the subject of the essay
THESIS STATEMENT	the writer's position about the topic

All writers must determine their purpose for writing; they must know what their main idea is and why it is important to them. This idea is contained in a special sentence called the **thesis statement.** The difference between a topic and a thesis statement is illustrated in the following example.

  Topic: cell phones in school

  Thesis statement: Student use of cell phones in schools should be prohibited.

Note that the topic does not usually show the writer's idea or position. However, the writer's opinion is clearly contained in the thesis statement.

Working on Thesis Statements

The most important sentence in an essay is the thesis statement. This statement identifies the writer's main idea and tells which points will be explained or supported in the body paragraphs of the essay. The thesis statement is a blueprint for the essay that follows.

Many excellent thesis statements include an idea about a topic and then a general reason to support that idea or position. For example, in "Against E-Voting," pages 2–3, the thesis statement clearly states the writer's position: "In particular, I believe that we should not vote with computers or other electronic media." The writer concludes the thesis statement by giving the reason to support this position: "because democracy is too important to cede to the unreliability of cyberspace."

NOTE: *Because* is followed by subject + verb; *because of* is followed by a noun. This structure is further explained in Grammar Topic 5.3 on page 126.

For each topic below, complete the thesis statement with an idea or a position in the first blank. Then add a controlling idea after the word because. *A controlling idea is a word or phrase that helps guide the flow of ideas in a paragraph or essay.*

1. Subject: Humanities / Topic: Authors / Thesis statement: My favorite author is _____

   because _____.

2. Subject: Sciences / Topic: Choice of study / Thesis statement: I want to study _____

   because _____.

3. Subject: Business / Topic: Plan of action / Thesis statement: If I could be the president of any company

   in the world, it would be _____ because _____.

4. Subject: Personal / Topic: Recreational activity / Thesis statement: My favorite recreational activity is

   _____ because _____.

For more practice with topics and thesis statements, try Unit 1, Activity 1 on the *Great Writing 5* Web site: elt.heinle.com/greatwriting

What Is in the Body of an Essay?

BODY	1. usually consists of three (or more) paragraphs 2. explains and supports the thesis statement

The **body** of an essay follows the introduction. In the body paragraphs, writers explain and support their ideas or the position they stated in the thesis statement. In a good essay, the body paragraphs develop the writer's thesis statement so that the reader fully comprehends the writer's point of view.

Transition Words

One way to make the supporting information in the body paragraphs clear is to use appropriate transition words. Transition words help the reader to follow the ideas in the essay. They can be single words, such as *but, this,* and *although.* Transitions can also be phrases, such as *in addition, as a result,* and *for these reasons.*

Two words that are especially helpful for connecting ideas in your writing are the adjectives *this* and *these.* You can mention an idea in one sentence and then refer to it in subsequent sentences using the words *this* and *these.* Using *this* or *these* helps readers to know that you are continuing to talk about the same topic. It is important to note that a noun is used with these two adjectives. The noun is usually a synonym or general noun for the idea that it is replacing or representing.

Examples from "Against E-Voting"

1. In Paragraph 2, the writer talks about the advantages of traditional voting systems. Paragraph 3 addresses the ways in which e-technologies can be exploited and thus circumvent honest voting practices. It is important to study how the writer moves from Paragraph 2 to Paragraph 3. The writer does not start talking directly about e-voting fraud in Paragraph 3. Instead, the writer says, "If *this* traditional system of voting is not used, however, voters do not really know whether their

votes are tallied accurately with e-voting systems." The word *this* is used as an adjective before the noun *system*. The word *system* has not been used before, but the writer is using the word *system* to represent the idea that was just explained.

2. In Paragraphs 2, 3, and 4, the writer explains why computer technologies create some serious problems. At the beginning of Paragraph 5, which is the conclusion, the writer argues that "*these technologies are not a panacea for all of society's troubles.*" Instead of repeating all the facts or reasons again, the writer uses the "umbrella" word *technologies* preceded by the adjective *these*.

 Writer's Note

Using *This* and *These* with Noun Synonyms

The purpose of *this, that, these,* and *those* is to connect information without repeating the same noun. Although these four words can function as pronouns or as adjectives, it is preferable to use them as adjectives in academic writing to ensure clarity. When you use *this* or *these* as an adjective, be sure to use a different noun—a synonym or general "umbrella" noun—instead of repeating the same noun. This strategy makes your writing sound more academic.

ORIGINAL NOUN

Hackers can gain access to many computer systems for illegal purposes.

TRANSITION WORD   SYNONYM

Good: **These criminals** could easily change the outcome of an election.

Weak: **These hackers** could easily change the outcome of an election.

Sometimes it is impossible to find a good synonym. In such cases, it is acceptable to repeat a noun once or twice. However, it is considered very weak writing to repeat the noun, so try to use a synonym.

ACTIVITY 3 *This* and *These*

Write this *or* these *on the line to show the second reference to a noun. The first one has been done for you.*

1. Submarines allow marine biologists to witness life in the ocean closely and to collect important data from these studies. _____*These*_____ vessels are an important resource for scientific study.

2. The flag of Libya is entirely green. _____ color is the national color of Libya.

3. In our history class today, we read about World War I. _____ war ended in 1918 and resulted in the deaths of millions.

4. The first step in making potato salad is to peel six potatoes. Once _____ step has been completed, you will boil the potatoes for fifteen minutes.

5. According to a report in the school newspaper yesterday, the president has suggested that university education be free for students who have a high grade point average. As expected, _____ proposal is extremely popular with the parents of _____ students. However, _____ story did not say how the president intends to pay for _____ plan.

For more practice with *this* and *these*, try Unit 1, Activity 2 on the *Great Writing 5* Web site: elt.heinle.com/greatwriting

What Does the Conclusion of an Essay Do?

CONCLUSION	1. restates the thesis statement (the writer's main point) 2. usually offers a suggestion, opinion, or prediction

Most good essays end with a **conclusion** that summarizes the writer's thesis statement. In the conclusion, a writer does not add any new information. In fact, the most common error that writers make in their conclusions is the addition of new information. Adding new information does not make your essay sound stronger or more convincing. Instead, new information may actually confuse your reader.

Good writers vary the content and style of their conclusions, but a conclusion often ends with a sentence that expresses a suggestion, an opinion, or a prediction. The writer suggests what should be done now, or the writer offers a final opinion about the topic, or the writer predicts what will happen next. The bottom line is that without a conclusion, essays often seem incomplete and unfinished.

Understanding the Writing Process: The Seven Steps

Step 1	Choose a topic.
Step 2	Brainstorm.
Step 3	Outline.
Step 4	Write the first draft.
Step 5	Get feedback from a peer.
Step 6	Revise the first draft.
Step 7	Proofread the final draft.

Step 1: Choose a Topic

Every essay addresses a specific topic, whether it is one that you choose or one that your teacher assigns. After the topic has been selected, your next task will be to develop ideas about that topic. In this explanation of the seven steps in the writing process, the topic that we will use is "technology in society" and the writer's thesis statement is "Computers have a negative influence on society."

Don't Write—THINK!

Many writers make the mistake of trying to write an essay without thinking. The first part of writing is not writing; it is thinking. If you start writing too soon, your essay will be unorganized and unfocused.

Think about your topic. What do you already know about it? What do your readers know about it? What do you need to find out about this topic? Only after you have completed this thinking process are you ready to begin writing.

Step 2: Brainstorm

The next step in writing an essay is to generate ideas about your topic by brainstorming. Study this example of brainstorming about the topic "technology in society." The student decided to focus on some negative influences to explain in the body paragraphs.

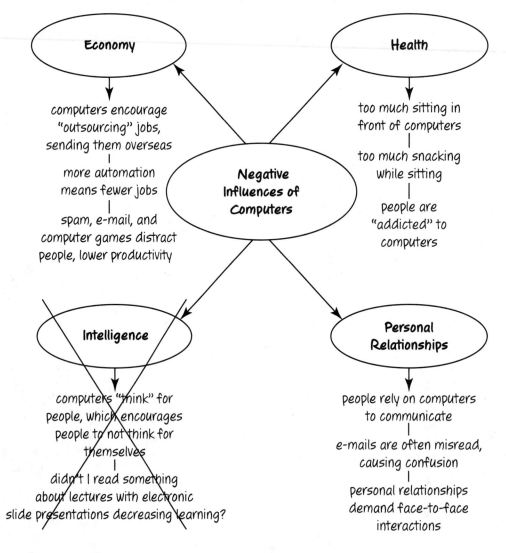

As you can see, the writer came up with four negative influences that computers have. She chose the three that she can present with the best support and crossed out the other.

Brainstorm in the box below about the following writing prompt: "Our government needs to enact, or put into practice, laws to control public use of foul (bad) language." When you are finished, compare your brainstorming with a partner's.

Brainstorming Box

Step 3: Outline

After you brainstorm your ideas, the next step is to make an outline. An outline helps you to organize how you will present your information. It helps you to see which areas of the essay are strong and which are weak.

Formal outlines use Roman numerals and capital letters. Some outlines consist of only words or phrases. Others have full sentences. Use the type of outline that will best help you write a great essay.

Here is an example of an outline that uses words, phrases, and sentences.

I. Introduction

    A. Hook (attention-getting sentence; see Writer's Note below)

    B. Background information

    C. Thesis statement: Computers have had a negative influence on society in three significant areas: personal relationships, health, and the economy.

II. Body Paragraph 1: Effects on personal relationships

    A. Topic sentence

    B. Effect 1

    C. Effect 2

III. Body Paragraph 2: Effects on health

    A. Topic sentence

    B. Effect 1

    C. Effect 2

IV. Body Paragraph 3: Effects on economy

    A. Topic sentence

    B. Effect 1

    C. Effect 2

V. Conclusion

    A. Restated thesis

    B. Brief discussion

    C. Prediction that with time, these three areas will steadily worsen if the situation continues

SUPPORT (marginal labels beside body paragraphs I, II, III)

Writer's Note

Using a Hook to Gain Readers' Attention

Good writers grab their readers' attention with the first sentence of an essay, which is called the **hook.** Just as people use a hook to catch fish, a writer will use a good hook to generate readers' interest in his or her essay.

Look at the two versions of a hook below for an essay about a vacation experience. The first hook, which uses the verb *be (was)*, is simple and boring. In contrast, the second hook gets the readers' attention by providing more details associated with the action verbs *catch, lose, get,* and *ruin*. Using specific verbs forces the writer to provide interesting details.

Boring hook (be verb): My worst vacation <u>was</u> in Switzerland.

Better hook (action verbs): It might seem unlikely to <u>catch</u> the flu, <u>lose</u> my wallet, and <u>get</u> a speeding ticket in the same week, but these incidents <u>ruined</u> my skiing vacation in Switzerland.

ACTIVITY 5 Outlining Practice

Read the outline of "Against E-Voting." Then use the information in the box to complete this outline for the essay.

- were based on simpler technologies
- should not be allowed to replace traditional voting technologies
- some problems but create other problems
- whether their votes are tallied accurately with e-voting
- and cons of this compromise position

I. Introduction

    A. Establish that computers are increasingly common in everyday life.

    B. Demonstrate that computers solve _____

    C. Thesis statement: We should not vote with computers or other electronic media.

II. Body Paragraph 1

    A. Establish that voting practices in the past _____

    B. These simpler technologies allow election results to be verified if there is an argument over the results.

III. Body Paragraph 2

    A. Explain that voters do not really know _____

    B. Discuss the threat that hackers pose to supposedly secure computer systems.

IV. Body Paragraph 3

    A. Address a possible compromise position, in which electronic voting machines provide a "receipt" of a person's vote.

    B. Discuss briefly the pros _____

SUPPORT (×3, in left margin)

V. Conclusion

    A. Discuss the ways in which technology cannot solve all human problems.

    B. Affirm position that e-voting _____

 Writer's Note

Peer Editing

A good way to generate ideas about improving your writing is to ask a friend or classmate to look at your organization, beginning with your outline. If something is not clear to the person reading your outline, then perhaps you should rework or rewrite that part. Sometimes information is not clear because there is a language problem. Other times, the problem is with a lack of good supporting points. Peer editing is commonly used for drafts, but it can also be useful for hooks and outlines and in every step in the writing process.

When you are editing someone else's work, remember to be helpful. If something is not clear, do not write "No." Such a simple remark is not helpful. You should write something more specific, such as, "This sentence is not clear" or "Can you think of three reasons to support this idea?"

The Peer Editing Sheets in Appendix 2 will help you to focus on specific areas to examine in each essay. Here are a few general things that a good peer editor looks for in essays:

- Does every sentence have a subject and a verb and express a complete thought?

- Are there any sentences or sections that do not make sense to you?

- Even if you do not agree with the writer's viewpoint, do you understand the writer's line of thinking?

Step 4: Write the First Draft

After you have completed your outline and received peer feedback on it, it is time to write the first draft of your essay. Writing an essay is never a linear process. As you write, you will make numerous changes. In fact, you may write the hook or other sentences, rewrite them, and later add additional words until the essay reaches its potential.

After you have brainstormed ideas for your essay, the next important step in writing a first draft is to put your ideas down on paper. After you have brainstormed, do not spend hours and hours thinking of what to write. A much better strategy is to get your ideas on paper and then edit your words to match what you really intend to say.

Step 5: Get Feedback from a Peer

Peer editing a draft is a critical step toward the final goal of a polished essay. As the writer of the essay, you will be helped by the fresh perspective a reader can give. It is often difficult for writers to see the weaknesses in their own writing.

Ask a colleague, friend, or classmate to read your essay and to offer suggestions about how to improve it. Some people do not like criticism, but constructive criticism is always helpful for writers. Remember that even professional writers have editors, so do not be embarrassed to ask for help.

Step 6: Revise the First Draft

Once you have received feedback from a reader, you can use that feedback to improve your essay in the second draft. You have four choices in responding to the feedback:

1. **Do nothing.** If you think the writing in your essay is clear enough, then do nothing. However, if one reader had a problem with an element in your essay, perhaps other readers will have the same problem.

2. **Add information.** If the reader found any unclear language or needed any parts clarified, then you might want to add more information. For example, you might need to add an adjective or identifying information, so instead of writing "the solution is actually quite easy," you could write, "the <u>best</u> solution <u>to this problem that plagues modern society</u> is actually quite easy."

3. **Edit.** If the reader found any grammatical errors, correct them. If your draft has errors with subject-verb agreement or preposition usage, then you should make corrections. For example, if you wrote, "Computers <u>has</u> had a negative impact <u>for</u> society in three significant <u>area</u>: personal relationships, health, <u>the</u> economy," you would edit the sentence in the underlined places to read, "Computers <u>have</u> had a negative impact <u>on</u> society in three significant <u>areas</u>: personal relationships, health, <u>and</u> the economy."

4. **Cut information.** If the reader thinks that your writing is wordy or that a certain sentence is not related to the topic, carefully consider his or her suggestions. If you agree with the reader's comments, then you should edit out the wordiness or omit the sentence.

Step 7: Proofread the Final Draft

Do not forget to proofread! When you proofread, you correct grammar and spelling errors. Careless mistakes make your writing look sloppy and get in the way of clear communication. Proofreading is not just about grammar and spelling, however. Even at this late stage, you can add or change words to make your essay sound better. It is essential to proofread your final essay carefully before you turn it in to your teacher.

 For more practice with essay structure, try Unit 1, Activity 3 on the *Great Writing 5* Web site: elt.heinle.com/greatwriting

This section contains grammar that may be review for you or that may be new. Grammatical errors in essays distract the reader and impede clear communication. Your goal should be to create error-free essays. This section will help you to become a better editor of your own writing. (NOTE: See the Brief Writer's Handbook with Activities, pages 194–198, for additional grammar activities.)

Grammar Topic 1.1
Nouns and Verbs

The most basic parts of speech are nouns and verbs. A **noun** names a person, place, feeling, or idea: *doctor, house, sadness, democracy.*

A **verb** is a word that shows an action or state of being: *run, write, think, be, do.*

It is often impossible to identify a word as a noun or verb until it is used in a sentence. Consider these examples with *book* and *cook.*

book as a noun:	She purchased a **book** about dinosaurs.
book as a verb:	When did you **book** your flight?

cook as a noun:	He is an excellent **cook.**
cook as a verb:	If you **cook** rice for too long, it will not taste good.

Certain endings usually indicate whether a word is a noun or a verb. Study the charts below.

Common Noun Endings	Example
-tion, -ion	instruction
-sion	conclusion
-ness	happiness
-ship	friendship
-er	teacher

Common Verb Endings	Example
-ate	donate
-ize	realize
-en	thicken
-ify	clarify
-ed	worked

Some word endings can be for nouns or verbs. For example, *-s* can indicate a plural noun or a third-person singular verb.

        VERB NOUN

He **books flights** for a living.

In addition, *-ing* can end a noun or a verb.

   NOUN   VERB

Swimming is her hobby. She is **swimming** in the pool now.

NOTE: See the Brief Writer's Handbook with Activities, pages 192–193, for more information on noun and verb endings.

Identify each group of words as N (nouns), V (verbs), or N/V depending on usage. The first one has been done for you.

1. __N__ writer, driver, server

2. _____ notify, rectify, beautify

3. _____ redden, widen, sadden

4. _____ conclusion, persuasion, confusion

5. _____ goodness, illness, awareness

6. _____ friendship, championship, scholarship

7. _____ died, cleaned, floated

8. _____ minimize, maximize, summarize

9. _____ dedicate, educate, infiltrate

10. _____ dedicated, educated, infiltrated

11. _____ dedication, education, infiltration

12. _____ dedicating, educating, infiltrating

Grammar Topic 1.2
Adjectives

Adjectives are words that describe nouns (or pronouns). Adjectives have many endings, but some common endings are *-y, -er* (meaning "more"), *-ed,* and *-ing.*

Common Adjective Endings	Example
-y	wind**y**
-er	cold**er**
-ed	tir**ed**
-ing	interest**ing**

NOTE: An important point to remember about adjectives is that when they accompany a noun, they are placed <u>before</u> the noun.

Incorrect: The thesaurus offers many synonyms and antonyms **interesting**.

Correct: The thesaurus offers many **interesting** synonyms and antonyms.

NOTE: See the Brief Writer's Handbook with Activities, page 192, for more information on adjective endings.

Circle the adjectives that modify the underlined nouns. Then write C or X to indicate if the word order is correct or incorrect.

_____ 1. Because of the confusing <u>address</u>, the package arrived late.

_____ 2. After completing her exam, the <u>student</u> Chinese left the room.

_____ 3. In the last election, the <u>candidate</u> Labor won by a small percentage.

_____ 4. We all agreed that Mark's wedding was an <u>event</u> elegant.

_____ 5. In Buenos Aires, most international <u>flights</u> do not depart early in the morning.

> For more practice with nouns, adjectives, and word order, try Unit 1, Activity 4 and Activity 5 on the *Great Writing 5* Web site: elt.heinle.com/greatwriting

Grammar Topic 1.3

Prepositions

Prepositions are words that show the relationship (often of place or time) between words in a sentence. Prepositions are usually small words, but they are important.

Common prepositions include *after, at, by, for, from, in, into, on, to, with,* and *without.*

A preposition and its noun or pronoun object are referred to as a prepositional phrase: *in May, with my aunt, to Mexico, for five minutes, after the meeting.*

In May , my parents took a trip to Seoul with my aunt .

NOTE: *To* + verb is not a prepositional phrase. It is the infinitive form of a verb: *to go, to swim, to write.*

Circle the prepositions in each sentence and underline the whole prepositional phrase. (Hint: The number in parentheses is the number of prepositional phrases in the sentence.) The first one has been done for you.

1. Everyone agrees that the greater efficiency (of) <u>computers</u> certainly offers us new possibilities (in) <u>so many areas</u> (of) <u>our lives</u>. (3)

2. Computers are beneficial, but they are tools, and we should not turn over all aspects of our lives to computers. (2)

3. In this particular instance, I believe that we should not vote with computers or other electronic media because democracy is too important to cede to cyberspace. (3)

4. Without this traditional system of voting, however, voters do not really know whether their votes are tallied accurately on e-voting systems. (3)

5. The simple fact is that hackers can gain access to many computer systems for illegal purposes. (2)

6. By illegally entering into a cyber-polling station, they could easily change the outcome of an election. (3)

 For more practice with prepositional phrases, try Unit 1, Activity 6 on the *Great Writing 5* Web site: elt.heinle.com/greatwriting

---

Grammar Topic 1.4
Confusing Words: Articles *A/An*

A and *an* are articles that come before nouns.

    a cat   an elephant

Sometimes an adjective comes between *a* or *an* and the noun it modifies.

    a <u>black</u> cat   an <u>interesting</u> cat

Use *an* before words that begin with a vowel sound.

    an <u>u</u>mbrella   an <u>o</u>pen door   an h<u>o</u>nest man

If a word begins with a vowel but not a vowel sound, do not use *an*. Instead, use *a*.

    a university   a uniform

ACTIVITY 9 Working with Confusing Words: Articles *A/An*

Fill in the blanks with a *or* an. *The first one has been done for you.*

An Outstanding Instructor

This paragraph is about Martha Nguyen. Mrs. Nguyen is (1.) __an__ English teacher at a local school. Everyone agrees that she is (2.) _____ outstanding teacher. She began her career as (3.) _____ teacher at Vietnam National University many years ago. After teaching there for five years, she decided to move to (4.) _____ nearby high school. She had many reasons for making this decision, but her primary motive was her desire to help young people write better. Mrs. Nguyen says that this move

was (5.) _____ very difficult decision but that it was (6.) _____ good one. She really enjoys her classes and her students. Her workload this semester is heavy. During this term, she is teaching four regular composition courses as well as (7.) _____ honors composition course. In the future, she may teach (8.) _____ university course on composition, but for the time being, she is quite happy as (9.) _____ teacher at the local school. I am certainly happy to be (10.) _____ student in her course this year.

Writer's Note

Watch Out for Word Parts!

Word parts include prefixes and suffixes. Prefixes come before the base word, and suffixes come at the end. Prefixes and suffixes change the meaning of the base word. For example, the prefix *un-* changes *happy* to *unhappy*. Suffixes affect the part of speech. For example, *-sion* and *-ment* are usually noun endings (*conclude/conclusion, enjoy/enjoyment*), while *-ent* and *-ish* are usually adjective endings (*differ/different, style/stylish*).

Mistakes with word parts, especially suffixes, are among the most common writing errors for student writers.

NOTE: See the Brief Writer's Handbook with Activities, pages 192–193, for more information on word parts.

Grammar Topic 1.5

Word Forms

Most people think of word forms as a vocabulary issue. Certainly, you can increase your vocabulary by understanding how other words are constructed with suffixes. However, one of the most common writing mistakes involves word forms. Recognizing word parts and using them correctly will improve your writing.

Read this joke. Five of the eight underlined words contain an error with word forms. Correct the error or write C (correct). If you need more information about word parts, review the Brief Writer's Handbook with Activities, pages 192–193. The first one has been done for you.

EXAMPLE PARAGRAPH

A Pizza Joke

One day, a young boy went to a pizza restaurant to get something to eat. The server said, "May I take your order?" The young boy said, "Yes, ma'am. I would like to order a cheese pizza." The server wrote down this (1.) informing ___*information*___, and then she asked what size pizza he (2.) wanted _____. Without (3.) hesitate _____, the young boy replied, "Please bring me a medium pizza." The (4.) serve _____ wrote this down, too, and then walked to the kitchen. A few minutes later, she came back and said, "I just (5.) realized _____ that I forgot to ask you something. The (6.) cooker _____ wants to know if you want your pizza cut into six or eight pieces." The young boy thought about this for a minute and then (7.) answer _____, "Well, I'm not that hungry, so just cut it into six pieces. I can't imagine (8.) eating _____ eight pieces of pizza."

Seven of the ten sentences contain an error involving one of the grammar topics featured in this unit. Write C before the three correct sentences. Write X before the incorrect sentences, circle the error, and write a correction above it.

_____ 1. The manager quickly realized that Abdullah had made a honest mistake.

_____ 2. Susan put the brown socks into the large suitcase.

_____ 3. The first word a sentence in begins with a capital letter.

_____ 4. My son's first pet was a huge cat.

_____ 5. The opposite of happiness is sad.

_____ 6. If you want to rectify this problem, you should call the company at once.

_____ 7. For travel international, it is necessary to have a valid passport.

_____ 8. The next train to Paris departs on six o'clock.

_____ 9. The invention of the telephone was certainly an event important in human history.

_____ 10. Please put the card into the machine for withdraw money.

ACTIVITY 12 Editing a Paragraph: Review of Grammar Topics 1.1-1.5

Seven of the ten underlined words or phrases in this paragraph contain an error involving one of the grammar topics featured in this unit. Correct the errors on the lines. If the word or phrase is correct, write C.

EXAMPLE PARAGRAPH

Confusing Homophones

One of the most (1.) <u>confuse</u> _____ aspects of the English language

is the use of homophones. What is (2.) <u>an</u> _____ homophone? Why do

homophones cause (3.) <u>confusion</u> _____ ? Homophones are (4.) <u>worded</u>

_____ that sound alike but are spelled differently. (5.) <u>In addition with</u>

_____ different spellings, the words usually have different origins. Examples

(6.) <u>inclusion</u> _____ *to/two/too; hour/our; knew/new; so/sew;* and *road/

rode.* To use the correct word (7.) <u>in</u> _____ the correct time, it is necessary

to know the (8.) <u>meaning</u> _____ of each of the homophones. We can write

"I have two books, too" but not "I have too books, two." Likewise, we can write "I rode on

the (9.) <u>bumpy road</u>" _____ but not "I road on the bumpy rode." (10.) <u>In

conclude</u> _____ , although they sound the same, homophones cannot be used

interchangeably.

Vocabulary is important in any writing. The following activities will help you improve your knowledge and application of better vocabulary. Activity 13 will help you build vocabulary word associations. Activity 14 will help you remember useful collocations, which are combinations of words.

ACTIVITY 13 Word Associations

Circle the word or phrase that is most closely related to the word or phrase on the left. If necessary, use a dictionary to check the meaning of words you do not know.

1.	technology	(a computer)	a briefcase
2.	efficiency	quick and fast	fancy and costly
3.	media	forms of communication	forms of traveling
4.	cyberspace	the World Wide Web	interplanetary exploration
5.	ballots	voting	swimming
6.	to ensure	to make certain	to make trouble
7.	tedious	energetic	time-consuming
8.	verifiable	able to correct	able to prove
9.	crucial	important	arrogant
10.	tallied	characterized	counted
11.	a scenario	a set of circumstances	a set of props
12.	paranoid	excessively kind	excessively fearful
13.	hackers	computer criminals	computer game players
14.	a receipt	proof of citizenship	proof of a transaction
15.	a panacea	a cure-all	an essay topic
16.	increasingly	to lower	to raise
17.	accurately	slowly	correctly
18.	reliable	affordable	dependable
19.	to omit	to exclude	to include
20.	the origin	the arrangement	the source

Collocations in Academic Writing

In addition to learning new vocabulary to improve the level of your academic writing, it is important to practice new vocabulary in examples that sound natural to academic writers. These natural combinations of words are called **collocations**.

Here are two examples of collocations that make the words sound more like advanced academic writing rather than like ordinary conversation:

Example 1: Consider which adjectives can go with the word *imagination* to mean "a very good imagination, the ability to imagine many different things."

> *Even from a very early age, she had a _____ imagination, which certainly led to her later artistic success.*
> (Suggested answer: *vivid*. Words such as *big* or *great* are possible, but they sound simplistic and ineffective in academic writing.)

Example 2: Consider which adjectives can go with the word *writer* to mean "producing a lot of works."

> *William Shakespeare, the great Renaissance playwright, was an extremely _____ writer, creating almost forty plays in his lifetime.*
> (Suggested answer: *prolific*. Words such as *busy* or *good* are not suitable for academic writing.)

ACTIVITY 14 Using Collocations

Fill in each blank with the word or phrase on the left that most naturally completes the phrase on the right. If necessary, use a dictionary to check the meaning of words you do not know.

1. do / make   to _____ a mistake

2. of / to   to turn over something _____ someone

3. process / part   for the most _____

4. event / means   the main _____ of transportation

5. from / by   to count votes _____ hand

6. improvement / security   a breach in _____

7. unlikely / quite   it is _____ possible

8. gain / take   to _____ access to

9. desire / way   to get in the _____ of something

10. change / technology   computer _____

11. of / in   all _____ society's troubles

12. constructive / information _____ criticism

13. money / time   to withdraw _____

14. complete / fulfill   to _____ a person's needs

15. tell / share   to _____ this information with everyone

16. in / on   to rely _____ someone or something

17. accomplishment / problem   this _____ plagues modern society

18. occurrence / process   a linear _____

19. date / instance   in this particular _____

20. mistake / problem   an honest _____

Original Student Writing: Essay

In this section, you will follow the seven steps in the writing process to write a five-paragraph essay. To review the details of each step, see pages 7–13.

ACTIVITY 15 Original Essay

Using the seven steps in the writing process that follow, write a five-paragraph essay.

Step 1: Choose a Topic

Your first step is to choose a topic for your essay. Your teacher may assign a topic, you may think of one yourself, or you may choose one from the suggestions below. As you consider possible topics, ask yourself, "What do I know about this topic? What do my readers know? What else do I need to know? Do I need to research this topic?"

Humanities	What are the advantages of being bilingual in today's society?
Sciences	Which twentieth-century scientific discovery caused the most change to our daily lives? Explain.
Business	Corporations have collapsed after top executives used dishonest accounting practices. What types of ethical reforms should be put in place to ensure that these practices end?
Personal	Describe your first trip to a zoo, theme park, or other tourist attraction.

1. What topic did you choose? _____

2. Why did you choose this topic? _____

_____

_____

Step 2: Brainstorm

Use this space to jot down as many ideas about the topic as you can.

Brainstorming Box

Step 3: Outline

Prepare a simple outline of your essay.

Title: _____

I. Introduction

   A. Hook: _____

     _____

   B. Connecting information: _____

     _____

     _____

   C. Thesis statement: _____

     _____

II. Body Paragraph 1

   A. Topic sentence: _____

     _____

   B. Supporting details: _____

     _____

SUPPORT

III. Body Paragraph 2

   A. Topic sentence: _____

     _____

   B. Supporting details: _____

     _____

SUPPORT

IV. Body Paragraph 3

   A. Topic sentence: _____

     _____

   B. Supporting details: _____

     _____

SUPPORT

V. Conclusion

   A. Restated thesis: _____

     _____

   B. Suggestion/opinion/prediction: _____

     _____

Peer Editing of Outlines

Exchange books with a partner. Read your partner's outline. Then use the following questions to help you to comment on your partner's outline. Use your partner's feedback to revise your outline.

1. Are the supporting paragraphs organized in a logical manner? If not, what suggestions do you have?

_____

_____

_____

2. Is there any aspect of the outline that looks unclear to you? Give details here.

_____

_____

_____

3. Which area of the outline could most benefit from further development? Give at least one specific suggestion.

_____

_____

_____

4. If you have any other ideas or suggestions, write them here.

_____

_____

_____

_____

Step 4: Write the First Draft

Use the information from Steps 1, 2, and 3 to write the first draft of your five-paragraph essay. Use at least five of the vocabulary words or phrases presented in Activity 13 and Activity 14. Underline these words and phrases in your essay.

Step 5: Get Feedback from a Peer

Exchange papers from Step 4 with a partner. Read your partner's writing. Then use Peer Editing Sheet 1 on page 209 to help you to comment on your partner's writing. Be sure to offer positive suggestions and comments that will help your partner improve his or her writing.

Step 6: Revise the First Draft

Read the comments on Peer Editing Sheet 1 about your essay. Then reread your essay. Can you identify places where you plan to make revisions? List the improvements that you are going to make.

1. _____

   _____

   _____

2. _____

   _____

   _____

3. _____

   _____

   _____

Use all the information from the previous steps to write the final version of your paper. Often, writers will need to write a third or even fourth draft to express their ideas as clearly as possible. Write as many drafts as necessary to produce a good essay.

Step 7: Proofread the Final Draft

Be sure to proofread your paper several times before you submit it.

Additional Topics for Writing

Here are ten topics for additional writing.

TOPIC 1: Explain why you would rather live in the city, in the suburbs, or in the country.

TOPIC 2: If you won $25,000, explain how you would spend it and why.

TOPIC 3: Who was your favorite elementary school teacher? Why?

TOPIC 4: If you could attend a major sports championship game, which would you choose to attend and why?

TOPIC 5: Do you want to have a large family when you are older? Why or why not?

TOPIC 6: Describe your best birthday ever. Why was this particular birthday special to you?

TOPIC 7: Which charity organization would you most like to support? Why?

TOPIC 8: What is your favorite TV program? Why do you like this program so much?

TOPIC 9: What was the best gift that you have given or received? What made this gift special?

TOPIC 10: If you were the mayor of your city, what law would you pass first? Why?

Timed Writing

How quickly can you write in English? There are many times when you must write quickly, such as on a test. It is important to feel comfortable during those times. Timed-writing practice can make you feel better about writing quickly in English.

First, read the essay guidelines below. Then take out a piece of paper. Read the writing prompt below the guidelines. As quickly as you can, write a basic outline for this writing prompt (including the thesis and your three main points). You should spend <u>no more than</u> 5 minutes on your outline.

You will then have 40 minutes to write a basic 5-paragraph essay about your topic. At the end of the 40 minutes, your teacher will collect your work and return it to you at a later date.

Essay Guidelines

- Remember to give your essay a title.

- Double-space your essay.

- Write as legibly as possible (if you are not using a computer).

- Include a short introduction (with a thesis statement), three body paragraphs, and a conclusion.

- Try to give yourself a few minutes before the end of the activity to review your work. Check for spelling, verb tense, and subject-verb agreement mistakes.

> If you could meet one famous person, living or dead, who would it be? Explain why you would choose to meet this person and what you would hope to gain from the experience.

Process Analysis Essays

GOAL: To learn how to write a process analysis essay

*Grammar Topics: 2.1 Subject-verb agreement; 2.2 Apostrophes; 2.3 Modals; 2.4 Confusing words: *you're/your*; 2.5 Word parts

What Is a Process Analysis Essay?

A **process analysis essay** explains in detail how a certain objective is accomplished. You might think of a process analysis essay as a set of instructions explaining the most effective means to achieve a desired result. The writer believes that the method he or she describes is the best way to accomplish the objective.

Although all process analysis essays describe how to accomplish a particular goal, the more interesting essays also include relevant information about the wider context of the process. Why is this process important? How is it useful to the reader who is learning about it? What are the benefits and/or limitations of the process? When you answer such questions as these before you write your essay, your writing will be better tailored to your specific audience.

When you write a process analysis essay, you need to pay special attention to your audience. Are your readers experts in the field? How much information do they need so that they can understand the process? For example, if you write an essay describing DNA splicing, it is quite important to know whether your readers are doctors of biology or high school freshmen.

How Is a Process Analysis Essay Organized?

The two most common ways of organizing a process analysis essay are **chronologically** and **by priority**.

- In a process analysis essay that is organized **chronologically,** the writer describes the steps in the order in which they should be performed. This method is helpful for teaching a person a new skill, such as how to cook rice or how to change the oil in a car.

- In a process analysis essay that is organized **by priority,** the writer organizes the steps in order of the most important to the least important. This method is useful for teaching a new concept, such as diplomacy in a foreign country.

Topics for Process Analysis Essays

What is a good topic for a process analysis essay? Process analysis essay topics can range from a task as simple as how to boil an egg to a task as complex as how to construct a house.

ACTIVITY 1 Identifying Topics for Process Analysis Essays

Read these eight topics. Put a check mark (✓) next to the four that could be good topics for process analysis essays.

_____ 1. the steps in applying for a bank loan to purchase a vehicle

_____ 2. Dubai versus Istanbul as a vacation destination

_____ 3. how to get a passport most efficiently

_____ 4. ways to convince citizens to support a candidate

_____ 5. an analysis of driving routes in a certain community

_____ 6. reasons for stopping smoking

_____ 7. an argument against illegal immigration

_____ 8. teaching children to paint

Think of two additional topics that would be appropriate for a process analysis essay.

9. _____

10. _____

For more practice with topics for process analysis essays, try Unit 2, Activity 1 on the *Great Writing 5* Web site: elt.heinle.com/greatwriting

Supporting Details

Many of the apparently simple things that we do every day, such as paying bills and cooking meals, involve processes with many steps. However, if you made a list of all of the actual steps in each process, you would quickly see that no process is really so simple.

ACTIVITY 2 Brainstorming Steps in a Process

Choose one of the following tasks and use the accompanying blank space to brainstorm the steps necessary to perform it. Then read your steps to a partner to check whether you included all of them.

1. directing someone to a building on the other side of campus

2. making your lunch

3. washing your clothes

4. taking care of your pet

Studying a Sample Process Analysis Essay

In this section, you will study three versions of a process analysis essay: a first draft, the same first draft with teacher comments, and the revised essay.

ACTIVITY 3 Warming Up to the Topic

Answer these questions individually. Then discuss them with a partner or in a small group.

1. What is the difference in meaning between *bargain* as a noun and *bargain* as a verb?

    _____

    _____

    _____

2. Have you ever bargained to buy something? Describe the experience.

    _____

    _____

    _____

3. What are two or three important things that you must do to bargain for the best price?

    _____

    _____

    _____

    What is one thing that you must avoid doing? _____

    _____

 For more practice with the structure of process analysis essays, try Unit 2, Activity 2 on the *Great Writing 5* Web site: elt.heinle.com/greatwriting

As you read this first draft, look for areas that need improvement.

ESSAY 2A

A Bargain

As we all know, bargaining is a **tough** business. The buyer wants to take a product at the lowest possible price. The seller wants to maximize the **potential** for **profit.** The desires of the buyer and the seller really oppose each other. It is in the best interest of these people to **strategize** exactly how they will convince a seller to low his prices. Although prices are **inflexible,** it never hurts to attempt to bargain with the seller.

Always assume that the price tag represents the starting point of you're negotiations, not the final word on the matter. I am usually very good at bargaining. You might to begin by asking the salesperson whether any sales or discounts will soon be announced. If you do not ask for a special deal, the salesperson probably will not **volunteer** to give you one. Since salespeople often **work on commission,** is frequently to their advantage to hide this information from you.

Another thing, you must be prepared to walk away from an item when you are bargaining. Even if you really want it. It's important that you never let sellers to know that you really want their products.

Finally, patience. Looking for bargains take the time and the energy. Sometime you might need to **break down** and buy a product at a more expensive price simply because you do not have the time necessary for shop any more. Whenever that happens, remember that your time is important, too, and sometimes it is worth spend a little extra money. Especially if you really desire the item.

A best **aspect** of bargain-hunting is that it is a lot of diversion, and at the same time, it is cheap. Why pay more in something you can buy for less? If you practice your bargaining skills often, you will **get better at** it and will have more money to bargain with the next time you go shopping.

tough: difficult

potential: capacity for growth, development, or coming into existence

profit: money made from a business activity

strategize: to make a plan of action

inflexible: rigid, refusing to change

volunteer: to give something of one's own free will

work on commission: to earn money in the form of a percentage of the cost of item sold instead of receiving the same amount of money, or salary, each pay period

break down: to stop resisting something

an aspect: a feature

get better at: to become good at, improve

Read the teacher comments on the first draft of "A Bargain." Are these the same things that you noticed?

This title does not express the content of your essay exactly

ESSAY 2B

A Bargain

If we all know this, you have no reason to write the essay

better: difficult process

wrong word choice

As we all know, bargaining is a tough business. The buyer wants to take a product

connect

at the lowest possible price. The seller wants to maximize the potential for profit.

poor word choice *combine*

The desires of the buyer and the seller really oppose each other. It is in the best

who? *make plural* *word form*

interest of these people to strategize exactly how they will convince a seller to low

sometimes

his prices. Although prices are inflexible, it never hurts to attempt to bargain with

the seller.

Add transition? *confusing words*

Always assume that the price tag represents the starting point of you're

Purpose of this sentence? Cut?

negotiations, not the final word on the matter. I am usually very good at bargaining.

You might to begin by asking the salesperson whether any sales or discounts will

better word: advertised

soon be announced. If you do not ask for a special deal, the salesperson probably

word missing

will not volunteer to give you one. Since salespeople often work on commission, is

frequently to their advantage to hide this information from you.

Add transition

Sounds like conversation Another thing, you must be prepared to walk away from an item when you are

fragment *no contractions*

bargaining. Even if you really want it. It's important that you never let sellers to know

You need more info here

that you really want their products.

fragment *S-V*

Finally, patience. Looking for bargains take the time and the energy. Sometime

you might need to break down and buy a product at a more expensive price simply

because you do not have the time necessary for shop any more. Whenever that

happens, remember that your time is important, too, and sometimes it is worth

fragment *wrong word*

spend a little extra money. Especially if you really desire the item.

article error ⟶ hunting for bargains

wrong word

Ⓐ best aspect of (bargain-hunting) is that it is a lot of (diversion,) and at the same

prep.

time, it is cheap. Why pay more (in) something you can buy for less? If you practice

your bargaining skills often, you will get better at it and ~~will~~ have more money to

bargain with the next time you go shopping.

Bargaining does not have a
cost, so it can't be cheap.

I enjoyed reading your content. You sound like a tough bargainer!
Good first draft. Your introduction and conclusion are good. Work on the title.
Work on paragraph 3—it needs more development. All body paragraphs
should begin with a transition. You must proofread your paper for fragments!
Three fragments in one essay are too many.

Read the revised version of the essay, now titled "Getting the Best Deal." What has been changed? What still needs improvement?

Getting the Best Deal

Bargaining is a difficult process. The buyer wants to purchase a product at the lowest possible price, but the seller wants to maximize the potential for profit. The desires of the buyer and the seller **unequivocally** oppose each other, and thus it is in the best interest of buyers to strategize exactly how they will convince sellers to lower their prices. Although prices are sometimes inflexible, it never hurts to attempt to bargain with the seller.

First, always assume that the price tag represents the starting point of your negotiations, not the final word on the matter. Assuming that the price tag is the final price of an item is the single worst mistake that a shopper can make in the bargaining process. You might begin by asking the salesperson whether any sales or discounts will soon be advertised. If you do not ask for a special deal, the salesperson probably will not volunteer to give you one. Since salespeople often work on commission, it is frequently to their advantage to hide this information from you.

Second, you must be prepared to walk away from an item when you are bargaining, even if you really want it. This step in the bargaining process requires determination and good acting skills, but it can pay off financially. It is important that you never let sellers know that you really want their products. At street markets and festivals, **scout out** the booths first to see whether anything interests you. If you go back to buy at the end of the day, the sellers will often give you discounts so that they will have fewer products to pack up.

Finally, be patient. Looking for bargains takes time and energy. Sometimes you might need to break down and buy a product at a more expensive price simply because you do not have the time necessary to shop any more. Whenever that happens, remember that your time is important, too, and sometimes it is worth spending a little extra money if you really want the item. However, if waiting two weeks or even two months saves you a **considerable** amount of money, then it is **worthwhile** to wait.

Hunting for bargains is a lot of fun, and at the same time, it can save you a great deal of money. Once you start bargaining, you may find that it becomes an addictive game in which you are competing with the salesperson for your money. If you practice your bargaining skills often, you will get better at it and have more money to bargain with the next time you go shopping.

---

unequivocally: without a doubt, clearly
scout out: to investigate

considerable: large, great
worthwhile: valuable, sensible

Analyzing Content and Organization

ACTIVITY 7 Analyzing the Content

Answer these questions about the revised version (Essay 2C) of "Getting the Best Deal."

1. Is this process analysis essay organized chronologically or by priority? _____

2. Why does the writer want to give advice about saving money?

   _____

3. Write the thesis statement here.

   _____

4. What specific suggestions does the writer offer about bargain hunting?

   _____

   _____

ACTIVITY 8 Analyzing the Organization

Read the outline of "Getting the Best Deal." Then use the information in the box to complete the outline for the essay.

• the end of the day	• effective bargaining skills
• patience	• the salesperson's interests
• successful bargaining	

I. Introduction

    A. Economics of shopping: both buyer and seller want to maximize profit.

    B. Thesis statement: _____ will help the

       reader to shop more effectively.

II. Body Paragraph 1

    A. Use the price tag as the starting point for negotiations, not as the final word on the price.

    B. _____ often are not the same as the buyer's.

III. Body Paragraph 2

    A. You should walk away from an item.

    B. Best to shop at _____

       1. Salespeople are tired.

       2. Salespeople want to make a final sale for the day.

SUPPORT

SUPPORT

IV. Body Paragraph 3

    A. Suggest that _____ is key to bargaining.

    B. Sometimes you need to stop bargaining and buy an item in order to save time.

V. Conclusion

    A. Indicate that _____ can be fun.

    B. Practice at bargaining helps you to get better and have more money for future bargaining.

✎ Writer's Note

Outlines

The purpose of an outline is to help you, the writer, organize your ideas and include sufficient and logical details that support your ideas. Some formal outlines contain only nouns or only full sentences, but some writers prefer to include nouns, phrases, sentences, or a mixture of these elements.

Note that the outline for "Getting the Best Deal" includes a mixture. If your instructor has not given you instructions for your outline, choose the system that is most comfortable for you.

Building Better Sentences

Correct and varied sentence structure is essential to the quality of your writing. For further practice with "Getting the Best Deal," go to Practice 2 on page 204 in Appendix 1.

Transitions and Connectors in Process Analysis Essays

The most commonly used transitions and connectors in process analysis essays are time words and phrases. A process analysis essay outlines the steps in achieving a goal, so the transitions that are needed are typically words and phrases that indicate sequence.

Transitions and Connectors Commonly Used in Process Analysis Writing		
after	finally	second
after that	first	soon
at first	immediately following	then
at the same time	last	third
before	later	until
during	meanwhile	when
eventually	next	while

ACTIVITY 9 Using Transitions and Connectors

Reread the revised version (Essay 2C) of "Getting the Best Deal" on pages 36–37. Find and list three transitions or connectors and write the paragraph number after each one.

1. Transition/connector: _____ Paragraph: _____

2. Transition/connector: _____ Paragraph: _____

3. Transition/connector: _____ Paragraph: _____

 For more practice with transitions for process analysis essays, try Unit 2, Activity 3 on the *Great Writing 5* Web site: elt.heinle.com/greatwriting

 # Building Better Grammar

This section will help you to refine your grammar skills and become a better editor of your own writing. (NOTE: See the *Brief Writer's Handbook with Activities*, pages 194–198, for additional grammar activities.)

Grammar Topic 2.1
Subject-Verb Agreement

In any sentence, the subject and verb must agree in number. This rule requires a singular verb to be used with a singular subject and a plural verb to be used with a plural subject.

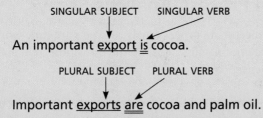

SINGULAR SUBJECT   SINGULAR VERB

An important <u>export</u> <u>is</u> cocoa.

PLURAL SUBJECT   PLURAL VERB

Important <u>exports</u> <u>are</u> cocoa and palm oil.

Words that come between the subject and the verb, such as a prepositional phrase, can sometimes cause writers to choose the wrong number for the verb. Remember that the object of a preposition is never the subject of a sentence.

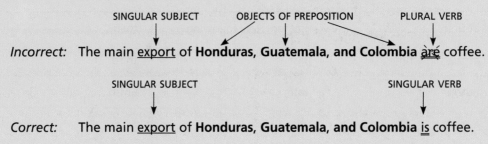

SINGULAR SUBJECT   OBJECTS OF PREPOSITION   PLURAL VERB

Incorrect: The main <u>export</u> of **Honduras, Guatemala, and Colombia** <u>are</u> coffee.

SINGULAR SUBJECT   SINGULAR VERB

Correct: The main <u>export</u> of **Honduras, Guatemala, and Colombia** <u>is</u> coffee.

Write the correct form of the verb in parentheses. Use the simple present tense.

1. After horrendous events, people often (react) _____ quite differently.

2. The secretary for our two departments (type) _____ over 75 words per minute.

3. Most of the countries in OPEC (export) _____ millions of dollars worth of petroleum each day.

4. Surprisingly, our company has found that a survey covering just five key colleges in the central part of the state often (reveal) _____ as much information as a survey of more than one hundred colleges.

5. The characters in Pearl Buck's *The Good Earth* (live) _____ very simple lives.

Grammar Topic 2.2
Apostrophes

The **apostrophe** (') has two main uses in English:

1. The apostrophe shows possession: *Susan's education, today's weather*

2. The apostrophe is used in contractions in place of a letter or letters that have been omitted: *can't (cannot), shouldn't (should not)*

Contractions are not common in academic writing. While it is acceptable to write *I'm* or *don't* in informal writing such as e-mails and notes, it is less acceptable in formal essays. One place where you might see contractions in essays, however, is in narrative writing. In assignments where you record your personal observations or reflections, such as in a journal or a reflective record, it may be acceptable and even preferable to use contractions such as *I've* or *I wasn't*. If you have any doubt about whether the use of contractions is acceptable in a written assignment, always ask your instructor for guidelines.

An extremely common error occurs when apostrophes are used to make plural forms. This usage is never correct.

Incorrect: For some writers, **apostrophe's** are difficult to understand.
Correct: For some writers, **apostrophes** are difficult to understand.

Contractions

> **Contractions** are not used in formal academic writing. However, jokes are usually told in informal spoken language—the kind of language used in conversation between friends—so a printed joke can have contractions to simulate spoken language. You will also see contractions in dialogs in novels or short stories where the author is trying to simulate spoken language.

ACTIVITY 11 Working with Apostrophes

Read this joke. Add apostrophes where necessary. Be prepared to explain your choices.

EXAMPLE PARAGRAPHS

The Lucky Dish

An antique collector with lots of money was walking in the downtown area of a city one day. He saw a small cat on the sidewalk in front of a store. The cat was drinking some milk from a small dish. The antique collector looked again at the dish. What the antique collector saw shocked him. The cats small dish was extremely old, and the antique dealer knew at once that the dish was very valuable. He was so interested in what he had just seen that he immediately walked into the store to talk to the owner about buying the valuable antique dish. The man did not want the owner to suspect that the dish was so valuable, so he offered the owner some money for the cat. He said that he would pay $10 for the cat. The owners answer shocked the man. "No," the owner said, "I couldnt ever sell this cat."

The man was getting desperate, so he offered the owner a crisp one-hundred-dollar bill from his wallet. At this point, the owner could no longer refuse what the man was offering. Then the man quickly added, "You know . . . how about including the dish, too? That cat is probably used to eating from that dish." The owner replied, "No, sir, Im sorry. You may be right about the cat and the dish, but that dish is not for sale." "Why not?" asked the man.

The owner answered, "Well, Ill tell you why its not for sale. You see, thats my lucky dish. I havent sold much merchandise, but so far this week, Ive sold four cats!"

Grammar Topic 2.3

Modals

Modals are words used with verbs to express ability, possibility, or obligation. Common modals include *can, could, may, might, must, should, will,* and *would.* Modals also include phrases, such as *ought to* and *had better.*

MODAL

I **should** take that writing class again.

The verb after a modal is always in the base, or simple, form with no inflected ending (*-ing, -ed, -en, -s*). In addition, do not put the word *to* between the modal and the verb.

Incorrect: The solution **might lies** in obtaining better raw materials.

Incorrect: The solution **might to lie** in obtaining better raw materials.

Correct: The solution **might lie** in obtaining better raw materials.

ACTIVITY 12 Working with Modals

Circle the six modals in this passage. Find the two errors and correct them.

EXAMPLE PARAGRAPH

A Trick for Remembering New Words

The task of learning and remembering new vocabulary words can be daunting. However, one technique that works for many students is the "key-word method." In this technique, learners must first to select a word in their native language that looks or sounds like the target English word. Then they should form a mental association or picture with the English word and the native-language word. For example, an English speaker learning the Malay word for *door, pintu,* might associating this target word with the English words *pin* and *into.* The learner would then visualize someone putting a "pin into a door" to open it. This could help the learner to remember *pintu* for *door.* Research on second-language learning shows that this technique consistently results in a very high level of learning.

Grammar Topic 2.4

Confusing Words: *You're/Your*

The words *you're* and *your* sound alike, but they are used very differently. Do not confuse them in your writing.

> *you're* = you are: **You're** planning to return these books to the library today.

> *your* = possessive adjective: Can you describe **your** new car to us?

ACTIVITY 13 Working with Confusing Words: *You're/Your*

Fill in the blanks with you're *or* your.

> ### EXAMPLE PARAGRAPH
>
> You know this situation well. (1.) _____ in (2.) _____ writing class.
> (3.) _____ teacher gives you (4.) _____ assignment. (5.) _____ to
> write an essay describing a process. Perhaps (6.) _____ not quite sure what you will use for
> your topic. What are (7.) _____ options? The topic of any process analysis essay must be
> one that entails steps. (8.) _____ essay should explain these steps. If (9.) _____
> successful at this, certainly (10.) _____ process analysis essay will be a good one.

Grammar Topic 2.5

Word Parts

You can increase your vocabulary in two basic ways. One way is to learn words that you have never seen before. The second way is to learn word parts, which will help you understand how other words are constructed. Recognizing word parts and using them correctly will increase your vocabulary and thus improve your writing.

NOTE: See the Brief Writer's Handbook with Activities, pages 192–193, for more information on word parts.

ACTIVITY 14 Editing Word Parts

Read the paragraph. Five of the eight underlined words contain an error with word parts. Correct the error or write C (correct).

Forms of Energy around Us

From the energy (1.) <u>expended</u> _____

by a hurricane or an earthquake to the energy (2.) <u>requirement</u>

_____ to make an automobile run,

energy affects our lives in ways that are impossible to ignore. Often,

when we talk about (3.) <u>energies</u> _____,

we are referring to the energy that people have channeled to provide

heat, light, and (4.) <u>powerful</u> _____

for homes and industries. As the sources we have (5.) <u>relied</u>

_____ on for this energy are depleted or are found to pose

(6.) <u>threatens</u> _____ to our environment, efforts to develop

(7.) <u>practical</u> _____ new sources are becoming

(8.) <u>intensification</u> _____.

ACTIVITY 15 Review of Grammar Topics 2.1–2.5

Seven of the ten sentences contain an error involving one of the grammar topics featured in this unit. Write C before the three correct sentences. Write X before the incorrect sentences, circle the error, and write a correction above it.

_____ 1. If you buy that sweater, your not going to be happy with it.

_____ 2. I do not know where Sammys' coat is; you should ask him.

_____ 3. Pamela thought that the move to Cozumel would be a wonderful change of pace, and she was certainly right.

_____ 4. He should does everything in his power to help out his friend.

_____ 5. Pandas eats a diet of bamboo shoots and leaves.

_____ 6. The politicians should all get behind this issue because they know that it will likely help them get reelected.

_____ 7. It is time for you to face the truth about you're responsibilities.

_____ 8. You're not going to heal if you keep taking the bandage off.

_____ 9. They might to want to help us with our problem since we might be able to help them with theirs.

_____ 10. Sitcoms was once very popular on television, but crime dramas are now the most popular shows.

ACTIVITY 16 Editing a Paragraph: Review of Grammar Topics 2.1–2.5

Seven of the ten underlined words in this paragraph contain an error involving one of the grammar topics featured in this unit. Correct the errors on the lines provided. If the word or phrase is correct, write C.

EXAMPLE PARAGRAPH

The Power of Listening

Listening is the communication skill that we most use. White-collar (1.) <u>workers'</u>

_____

typically devote at least 40% of their workday to listening. Yet immediately after hearing a ten-minute oral presentation, the average person (2.) <u>retain</u>

_____ only 50% of the information. Forty-eight hours later, only 25% of what was heard can be recalled. Thus, listening is probably the least developed of the four verbal communication skills (writing, reading, speaking, and listening). The good news (3.) <u>are</u>

_____ that you (4.) <u>can improve</u> _____

(5.) <u>your</u> _____ listening skills. Tests at the University of Minnesota

(6.) <u>shows</u> _____ that (7.) <u>individual's</u> _____

who receive training in listening improve their listening skills by 25% to 42%. To learn to listen more effectively, whether (8.) <u>your</u> _____ involved in a one-on-one

dialog or (9.) <u>are</u> _____ part of a mass audience, give the speaker your undivided attention, stay open-minded, avoid interrupting, and (10.) <u>involvement</u>

_____ yourself in the act of communication.

Building Better Vocabulary

Circle the word or phrase that is most closely related to the word or phrase on the left. If necessary, use a dictionary to check the meaning of words you do not know.

1.	bargaining	buying	producing
2.	to maximize	to make bigger	to make more difficult
3.	potential	practicality	possibility
4.	desires	wishes	fears
5.	unequivocally	completely	almost
6.	to strategize	to plan	to capitulate
7.	to convince	to lose	to persuade
8.	inflexible	soft	firm
9.	to attempt	to formulate	to try
10.	negotiations	discussions	commands
11.	discounts	lower prices	higher prices
12.	to volunteer	to decline	to offer
13.	a commission	a payment	a bribe
14.	festivals	celebrations	sufferings
15.	to scout	to smell	to hunt
16.	a booth	a stall	a mistake
17.	products	merchandise	leftovers
18.	expensive	cheap	costly
19.	worthwhile	time-consuming	valuable
20.	to entail	to conclude	to include

ACTIVITY 18 Using Collocations

Fill in each blank with the word or phrase on the left that most naturally completes the phrase on the right.
If necessary, use a dictionary to check the meaning of words you do not know.

1. at / in   to purchase a product _____ the lowest price possible

2. about / for   potential _____ profit

3. another / other   to oppose each _____

4. of / with   in the best interest _____ buyers

5. around / with   to bargain _____

6. of / after   the starting point _____ your negotiations

7. on / under   the final word _____ the matter

8. whether / that   to ask the salesperson _____

9. for / over   if you do not ask _____ a special deal

10. in / on   to work _____ commission

11. around / from   to hide this information _____ you

12. away / to   to walk _____ from

13. out / forth   to scout _____

14. of / in   at the end _____ the day

15. for / in   looking _____ bargains

16. at / in   _____ a more expensive price

17. at / on   _____ the same time

18. of / on   a lot _____ money

19. cost / price   a _____ tag

20. marketed / minded open- _____

Original Student Writing: Process Analysis Essay

In this section, you will follow the seven steps in the writing process to write a process analysis essay. To review the details of each step, see Unit 1, pages 7–13.

ACTIVITY 19 Original Process Analysis Essay

Using the seven steps that follow, write a process analysis essay.

Step 1: Choose a Topic

Your first step is to choose a topic for your essay. Choose a process that you can explain because you know the steps well. Your teacher may assign a topic, you may think of one yourself, or you may choose one from the suggestions below. As you consider possible topics, ask yourself, "What do I know about this topic? What do my readers know? What else do I need to know? Do I need to research this topic?"

Humanities	Write a process analysis essay in which you describe how to write a poem, research a subject in the library, or teach an academic lesson to a group of high school students.
Sciences	Scientists often write process analysis papers describing how they achieved a particular set of results from an experiment. Write a process analysis essay describing an experiment so that someone could duplicate your results.
Business	Managers often codify business practices so that standard procedures will be followed across the company. Write a process analysis essay describing the necessary procedure for a key function of a business in which you have been involved, such as advertising, marketing, or selling a product.
Personal	Think of your favorite hobby. How would you explain it to a friend who is interested in learning about it? Write a process analysis essay in which you describe the rudimentary skills necessary for your favorite hobby.

1. What topic did you choose? _____

2. Why did you choose this topic? _____

_____

_____

3. How well do you know this topic? What is your experience with it?

_____

_____

Step 2: Brainstorm

Use this space to jot down as many ideas about the topic as you can.

Brainstorming Box

Step 3: Outline

Prepare a simple outline of your essay.

Title: _____

I. Introduction

   A. Hook: _____

   _____

   B. Connecting information: _____

   _____

   _____

   C. Thesis statement: _____

   _____

II. Body Paragraph 1

SUPPORT

A. Topic sentence: _____

_____

B. Supporting details: _____

_____

III. Body Paragraph 2

SUPPORT

A. Topic sentence: _____

_____

B. Supporting details: _____

_____

IV. Body Paragraph 3

SUPPORT

A. Topic sentence: _____

_____

B. Supporting details: _____

_____

V. Conclusion

A. Restated thesis: _____

_____

B. Suggestion/opinion/prediction: _____

_____

Peer Editing of Outlines

Exchange books with a partner. Read your partner's outline. Then use the following questions to help you to comment on your partner's outline. Use your partner's feedback to revise your outline.

1. Is there any aspect of the outline that looks unclear to you? Give details here.

_____

_____

_____

2. Can you think of an area in the outline that needs more development? Do you have any specific suggestions?

_____

_____

_____

3. If you have any other ideas or suggestions, write them here.

_____

_____

_____

Step 4: Write the First Draft

Use the information from Steps 1, 2, and 3 to write the first draft of your process analysis essay. Use at least five of the vocabulary words or phrases presented in Activity 17 and Activity 18. Underline these words and phrases in your essay.

Step 5: Get Feedback from a Peer

Exchange papers from Step 4 with a partner. Read your partner's writing. Then use Peer Editing Sheet 2 on page 211 to help you to comment on your partner's writing. Be sure to offer positive suggestions and comments that will help your partner improve his or her writing.

Step 6: Revise the First Draft

Read the comments on Peer Editing Sheet 2 about your essay. Then reread your essay. Can you identify places where you plan to make revisions? List the improvements you are going to make.

1. _____

_____

2. _____

_____

3. _____

_____

Use all the information from the previous steps to write the final version of your paper. Often, writers will need to write a third or even fourth draft to express their ideas as clearly as possible. Write as many drafts as necessary to produce a good essay.

Step 7: Proofread the Final Draft

Be sure to proofread your paper several times before you submit it.

Writer's Note

Tip for Better Proofreading

One suggestion for better proofreading is to read your essay aloud. Reading aloud forces you to read more slowly, so you have a better chance of spotting your errors. You will be surprised at how many errors you can find by following this simple advice.

Additional Topics for Writing

Here are ten topics for additional process analysis essay writing.

TOPIC 1: Explain how to study a new language.

TOPIC 2: Explain the process of finding volunteer work.

TOPIC 3: What are the steps in becoming accustomed to a new job?

TOPIC 4: Explain how to settle a dispute between two friends.

TOPIC 5: Explain how to plan for a vacation.

TOPIC 6: Explain how to find free time for yourself during a busy day.

TOPIC 7: Describe how to monitor the performance of employees.

TOPIC 8: Explain the steps to follow to invest in the stock market.

TOPIC 9: Explain the steps in learning a new hobby.

TOPIC 10: Describe how to apply for a job.

Timed Writing

How quickly can you write in English? There are many times when you must write quickly, such as on a test. It is important to feel comfortable during those times. Timed-writing practice can make you feel better about writing quickly in English.

First, read the essay guidelines below. Then take out a piece of paper. Read the writing prompt below the guidelines. As quickly as you can, write a basic outline for this writing prompt (including the thesis and your three main points). You should spend <u>no more than</u> 5 minutes on your outline.

You will then have 40 minutes to write a 5-paragraph process analysis essay about your topic. At the end of the 40 minutes, your teacher will collect your work and return it to you at a later date.

Process Analysis Essay Guidelines

- Determine the multiple steps that make up the process that will be discussed in the essay.

- Make sure that each step receives adequate attention.

- Use transitions appropriately to help your readers move from one step to the next.

- Remember to give your essay a title.

- Double-space your essay.

- Write as legibly as possible (if you are not using a computer).

- Include a short introduction (with a thesis statement), three body paragraphs, and a conclusion.

- Try to give yourself a few minutes before the end of the activity to review your work. Check for spelling, verb tense, and subject-verb agreement mistakes.

> How do you prepare for final exams? Explain the process of studying for exams to a student four years younger than you.

Comparison Essays

GOAL: To learn how to write a comparison essay

*Grammar Topics: **3.1** Comparative forms (-er, more / less; as . . . as, the same . . . as); **3.2** Parallel comparison; **3.3** Non-count nouns; **3.4** Confusing words: than/then; **3.5** Word parts

What Is a Comparison Essay?

A **comparison essay** analyzes how two related subjects are similar and different. For example, you might select Julius Caesar and Alexander the Great for an essay on historical military figures. You could choose to write a comparison essay on the car and the bicycle as forms of urban transportation. Sometimes the writer includes an opinion about the merits of the subjects being compared.

The subjects that you compare should have some characteristics in common. Have you ever heard the phrase "You should not compare apples to oranges"? This expression suggests that it is best to compare and contrast similar objects. For example, you could write a comparison essay about the differences between a politician and a movie star. However, unless the movie star is running for office (or unless the politician is auditioning for a movie), it is hard to see the purpose of the comparison. On the other hand, a comparison essay that addresses which of two candidates running for office a voter should support or which of two actors should be cast in a certain role would have a much more unified focus and a stronger thesis because there is a reason to compare and contrast the two.

Some comparison essays suggest that a particular subject is better than another. As you will see, the sample essay in this unit models an opposing style in which the writer does not argue that one subject is better than another. Instead, the writer offers a thesis about the value of comparing and contrasting two animals.

A comparison essay can do one of three things:

- It can say that the two subjects are more different than similar.

- It can say that the two subjects are more similar than different.

- It can show how the two subjects share both similarities and differences.

In other words, your essay may focus on comparing, on contrasting, or on both.

How Is a Comparison Essay Organized?

There are two basic ways to organize a comparison essay: **block method** and **point-by-point method.** Both styles have an introduction and a conclusion, but the body paragraphs are organized differently.

The Block Method

In the block method, you present information about one subject first and then present information about the other subject. The number of paragraphs that you use for each subject separately should be the same. The block method looks like this:

INTRODUCTION	Paragraph 1	Hook, connecting information, thesis
BODY	Paragraph 2	Subject A • Point 1 • Point 2 • Point 3
	Paragraph 3	Subject B • Point 1 • Point 2 • Point 3
	Paragraph 4	Compares or contrasts Subject A and Subject B side by side
CONCLUSION	Paragraph 5	Restated thesis, suggestion/opinion/prediction

The Point-by-Point Method

In the point-by-point method, one point for comparison is the topic for each body paragraph. The writer discusses both subjects in relation to that one point. The point-by-point method looks like this:

INTRODUCTION	Paragraph 1	Hook, connecting information, thesis
BODY	Paragraph 2	Point 1 • Subject A • Subject B
	Paragraph 3	Point 2 • Subject A • Subject B
	Paragraph 4	Point 3 • Subject A • Subject B
CONCLUSION	Paragraph 5	Restated thesis, suggestion/opinion/prediction

Topics for Comparison Essays

What is a good topic for a comparison essay? Obviously, it should be two subjects that are related in some way. You must have a logical reason for making the comparison or contrast. What features do the subjects have in common? What features do they not share? Can you develop a thesis by comparing and contrasting their traits?

Here are some general topics that lend themselves well to a comparison essay:

- your siblings
- your favorite singers
- your favorite TV shows
- courses of study at two different colleges
- two authors who write on a similar topic

- vegetarian and nonvegetarian diets
- two local newspapers
- political parties
- your favorite vacation spots
- two ways of thinking about a topic

ACTIVITY 1 Identifying Topics for Comparison Essays

Read these eight topics. Put a check mark (✓) next to the four that could be good topics for comparison essays.

_____ 1. the steps in applying for a bank loan to purchase a vehicle

_____ 2. Rio de Janeiro versus Barcelona as a vacation destination

_____ 3. buying an SUV or a sedan

_____ 4. life with or without a baby in the house

_____ 5. an analysis of voting trends in recent Kenyan elections

_____ 6. the career choice of becoming a teacher or a lawyer

_____ 7. fun activities during a snowstorm

_____ 8. the migratory routes of penguins

Think of two additional topics that would be appropriate for a comparison essay.

9. _____

10. _____

Supporting Details

After you have selected a topic and the two subjects, your job is to identify the similarities and differences between the two subjects. This process will also help you to identify supporting details for your essay.

Think about two people, places, or things that could be compared and contrasted. Fill in the general topic, the two items, and lists of their similarities and differences. When you have finished, discuss your ideas with a partner. Then do the same for another pair of items. One example has been provided.

General Topic	Subject A	Subject B	Similarities	Differences
1. my parents	my mom	my dad	1. age 2. food likes/dislikes 3. attitude toward saving money	1. hobbies 2. attention to detail 3. showing affection 4. superstitious
2.				
3.				

Studying a Sample Comparison Essay

In this section, you will study three versions of a comparison essay: a first draft, the same first draft with teacher comments, and the revised essay.

ACTIVITY 3 Warming Up to the Topic

Answer these questions individually. Then discuss them with a partner or in a small group.

1. What is a stereotype? _____

   _____

2. Choose a general noun, such as *profession*. Think of categories within that general noun—*librarians, police officers, lawyers*. Then come up with three stereotypes about the category words, such as *Most librarians are serious people.*

   General noun: _____

Category	Stereotype
a. _____	a. _____
_____	_____
b. _____	b. _____
_____	_____
c. _____	c. _____
_____	_____

3. Do you have a pet or know someone who has a pet? What kind of animal is it? How would you describe the pet's character and personality? _____

   _____

   _____

   _____

4. Two popular pets are cats and dogs. What are the stereotypes of a cat? _____

   _____

   _____

   What are the stereotypes of a dog? _____

   _____

   _____

5. On the basis of your experience, do you think these stereotypes are accurate? Why or why not?

_____

_____

_____

_____

_____

_____

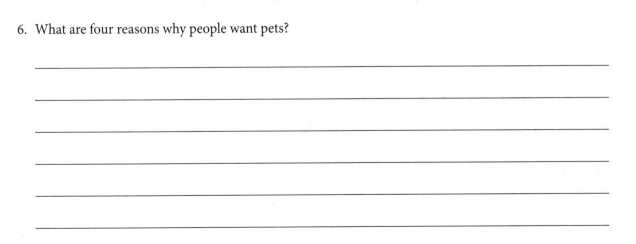

6. What are four reasons why people want pets?

_____

_____

_____

_____

_____

_____

As you read this first draft, look for areas that need improvement.

The Truth about the Cats and the Dogs

I used to think that the dogs were better then the cats as pets. As I was grow up, my family had a lot of the dogs—many kinds—but we never had cats because my father is allergic to it. I always assumed that when I grew up, I would to have a dog as a pet. My life as a pet owner changed one night when the tiny kitten **showed up** at my door. He was cold, wet, and hungry, and I was afraid him would die on my doorstep if I did not help him. I never saw myself as a cat owner, but now that I am one, I realize that most of the **stereotypes** about the cats and the dogs are lies.

The cats are suppose to be not good as well as not nice. My cat, however, are very friendly and even a little messy. He always want my attention, which can be annoying at times. I thought that a cat would sleep all day, but my cat is much more energetic then I expected. If he does not go outside to make **frolic** in the backyard, he starts to behave a bit **neurotically.**

The people also say that the dogs are more friendlier than the cats, but I remember a couple of the dogs of my family that were not friendly at all. Our Chihuahua was named "Wagster," and he did not like anyone. Every time someone rang our doorbell, he would to bark greatly to scare the visitor away. Once he even bit a little my grandmother! She never thought that the dogs were friendly after that experience.

My friend Aimee had a cat that was so **aloof** and distant that I never saw it when I came to visit. When I **dropped by** her house, the cat always hid itself under a bed.

My friend Jasper has a dog named Bono that is almost very friendly. Whenever I visit my friend, Bono runs up to me and tries to jump on me. He's so friendly. In fact, I wish he were not quite so friendly. Jasper does not live in my hometown now, and he probably does not have any pets now.

How did this stereotypes about the cats and the dogs develop? As with most **prejudices,** they reflect more about the peoples who express them than about what is true. Both the cats and the dogs make good pets, and they are bad. It all depends on the individual animal.

show up: to appear, often unexpectedly
a stereotype: a conventional or oversimplified idea or image of something
frolic: to play, as a young child or young animal
neurotically: in an unreasonable way

aloof: distant, reserved, or indifferent in manner
drop by: to visit, usually unexpectedly or informally
a prejudice: an unfair judgment or opinion formed before one knows the facts

Read the teacher comments on the first draft of "The Truth about the Cats and the Dogs." Are these the same things that you noticed?

Don't use THE unless specific—You have many errors like this. I didn't mark them all.

The Truth about the Cats and the Dogs   *Edit carefully!*

I used to think that the dogs were better ~~then~~ the cats as pets. As I was

List examples—reader needs details grow up, my family had a lot of the dogs—many kinds—but we never had cats

because my father is allergic to it. I always assumed that when I grew up, I would to

have a dog as a pet. My life as a pet owner changed one night when the tiny kitten

showed up at my door. He was cold, wet, and hungry, and I was afraid him would die

on my doorstep if I did not help him. I never saw myself as a cat owner, but now that

too strong—better word: untrue
I am one, I realize that most of the stereotypes about the cats and the dogs are lies.
Use your dictionary—these are beginning level adjectives.   Push yourself!

The cats are suppose to be not good as well as not nice. My cat, however,

S-V
are very friendly and even a little messy. He always want my attention, which

Details: give an example or two of the times
can be annoying at times. I thought that a cat would sleep all day, but my cat

is much more energetic then I expected. If he does not go outside to make
FROLIC is a verb
frolic in the backyard, he starts to behave a bit neurotically.

word form
The people also say that the dogs are more friendlier than the cats, but I
use possessive form
remember a couple of the dogs of my family that were not friendly at all. Our

Chihuahua was named "Wagster," and he did not like anyone. Every time someone

word choice
rang our doorbell, he would to bark greatly to scare the visitor away. Once he even
word choice—dictionary!
bit a little my grandmother! She never thought that the dogs were friendly after

that experience.

My friend Aimee had a cat that was so aloof and distant that I never saw it when

I came to visit. When I dropped by her house, the cat always hid itself under a bed.

My friend Jasper has a dog named Bono that is almost very friendly. Whenever

I visit my friend, Bono runs up to me and tries to jump on me. He's so friendly.

In fact, I wish he were not quite so friendly. Jasper does not live in my hometown

now, and he probably does not have any pets now.

How did this stereotypes about the cats and the dogs develop? As with most

prejudices, they reflect more about the peoples who express them than about what is

true. Both the cats and the dogs make good pets, and they are bad. It all depends on

the individual animal.

Cats vs. Dogs—this is the dilemma that pet owners face. I enjoyed reading your essay, which tries to debunk the stereotypes about these two animals.

Your ideas are expressed relatively clearly, but to improve this essay, you must raise the level of your vocabulary. A good writer avoids bland words such as NICE and GOOD. Use more specific adjectives.

Paragraph 4 needs work.

The conclusion is solid in content but needs better language.

Read the revised version of the essay, now titled "The Truth about Cats and Dogs." What has been changed? What still needs improvement?

The Truth about Cats and Dogs

I used to think that dogs were better than cats as pets. As I was growing up, my family had a lot of dogs—**mutts,** poodles, Chihuahuas, dachshunds—but we never had cats because my father is allergic to them. I always assumed that when I grew up, I would have a dog as a pet. My life as a pet owner changed one night when a tiny kitten showed up at my door. He was cold, wet, and hungry, and I was afraid he would die on my doorstep if I did not help him. I never saw myself as a cat owner, but now that I am one, I realize that most of the stereotypes about cats and dogs are untrue.

Cats are supposed to be **standoffish** and disinterested as well as **finicky** and **meticulous**. My cat, however, is very friendly and even a little messy. He always wants my attention, which can be annoying at times, especially when I am trying to cook or study. I thought that a cat would sleep all day, but my cat is much more energetic than I expected. If he does not go outside to frolic in the backyard, he starts to behave a bit neurotically. Obviously, my cat does not fit the stereotype of the average cat.

People also say that dogs are friendlier than cats, but I remember a couple of my family's dogs that were not friendly at all. Our Chihuahua was named Wagster, and he did not like anyone. Every time someone rang our doorbell, he would bark

ferociously to scare the visitor away. Once he even **nipped** at my grandmother! She never thought that all dogs were friendly after that experience. We also had another dog named Rover that used to bark loudly whenever the postal carrier came to deliver our mail. Even though our carrier never met our dog, I am certain that he knew that Rover was not a very friendly dog.

Of course, I have known both cats and dogs that **fulfill** the stereotypes as well. My friend Aimee had a cat that was so aloof and distant that I never saw it when I came to visit. No matter how many times I dropped by her house, the cat always hid itself under a bed. Likewise, my friend Jasper has a dog named Bono that is almost ridiculously friendly. Whenever I visit my friend, Bono runs up to me and tries to jump on me. He's so friendly. In fact, I wish he were not quite so friendly.

How did these stereotypes about cats and dogs develop? As with most prejudices, they reflect more about the people who express them than about what is true. Both cats and dogs make good pets, and both of them can make bad pets. It all depends on the individual animal, and no one should judge an animal before getting to know it.

a mutt: a dog of mixed breed
standoffish: unfriendly, aloof
finicky: very fussy, hard to please
meticulous: extremely careful and precise

ferociously: savagely, fiercely
nip: to grab and bite
fulfill: to make real

Analyzing Content and Organization

Answer these questions about the revised version (Essay 3C) of "The Truth about Cats and Dogs."

1. What is the topic of the essay? _____

2. What is the writer's thesis? _____

_____

3. What are some features of cats that the writer discusses?

_____

_____

4. What are some features of dogs that the writer discusses?

_____

_____

5. According to the writer, what are common stereotypes about cats?

_____

_____

6. Write one detail that supports the thesis statement.

_____

_____

7. This essay is organized by *(circle one)*:　　　block method　　　point-by-point method

---

 ## Writer's Note

Used To + Verb

You know several ways to express past tense in English, including the simple past tense, past perfect tense, and past progressive tense.

simple past tense:	Mia **talked** to her sister last night.
past perfect tense:	She **had talked** to her sister the day before yesterday, too.
past progressive tense:	She got another call while she **was talking** to her sister.

Another way to express an action in the past is with *used to*. We use *used to* + verb to describe an action that happened in the past many times but is no longer true.

When I was a child, I **used to** <u>hate</u> onions, but now I eat them on salads all the time.

Use *used to* + verb as a special way to say that something happened (repeatedly) in the past but is unlikely to happen again. We do not use *used to* + verb to express an action that happened only once, did not happen repeatedly, or will probably happen again.

Incorrect: When I was in Paris last week, I **used to see** the Eiffel Tower.

Correct: When I was in Paris last week, I **saw** the Eiffel Tower.

ACTIVITY 8 Analyzing the Organization

Read the outline of "The Truth about Cats and Dogs." Then use information in the box to complete the outline.

> - common stereotypes about dogs
> - many stereotypes about cats and dogs are untrue
> - the people who express them
> - a cat that fulfills feline stereotypes
> - an example of a cat that defies these stereotypes

I. Introduction

   A. Describe my previous beliefs about pets.

   B. Tell what my plans for pet ownership were and how they changed.

   C. Thesis statement: _____

II. Body Paragraph 1

   A. Discuss common stereotypes about cats.

   B. Provide _____

III. Body Paragraph 2

   A. Discuss _____

   B. Provide an example of a dog that defies these stereotypes.

IV. Body Paragraph 3

   A. Provide an example of _____

   B. Provide an example of a dog that fulfills canine stereotypes.

V. Conclusion

   A. Suggest that stereotypes reveal more about _____ than the actual truth.

   B. Conclude that both cats and dogs make good pets.

✎ Building Better Sentences

Correct and varied sentence structure is essential to the quality of your writing. For further practice with "The Truth about Cats and Dogs," go to Practice 3 on page 205 in Appendix 1.

Transitions and Connectors in Comparison Essays

Transitions and connectors are important in comparison essays; they help make clear the relationship between ideas about the two subjects. This is particularly true in the point-by-point method. In the block method, the subject being discussed is clear because the whole paragraph is about that one subject. However, when the point-by-point method is used, both subjects are discussed in relation to each point. Precise use of transitions helps the reader to follow the writer's comparisons.

Transitions and Connectors That Focus on Similarities			
also	compared to	like	similar to
as	have in common	likewise	similarly
as well (as)	in the same way	(the) same as	too
both			

Transitions and Connectors That Focus on Differences			
although	even though	on the other hand	unlike
but	however	(the) opposite	whereas
contrary to	in contrast (to)	(the) reverse	while
contrasted with	instead	though	yet
(X) differs (from Y)	on the contrary	unless	

 For more practice with structure of comparison essays, try Unit 3, Activity 1 on the *Great Writing 5* Web site: elt.heinle.com/greatwriting

ACTIVITY 9 Using Transitions and Connectors

Reread the revised version (Essay 3C) of "The Truth about Cats and Dogs" on pages 64–65. Find and list six transitions or connectors and write the paragraph number after each one. The first one has been done for you.

Transitions/Connectors That Show Similarity		Transitions/Connectors That Show Differences	
1. _____ also _____	(3)	1. _____	( )
2. _____	( )	2. _____	( )
3. _____	( )		
4. _____	( )		

 For more practice with transitions in comparison essays, try Unit 3, Activity 2 on the *Great Writing 5* Web site: elt.heinle.com/greatwriting

⟍ Building Better Grammar

This section will help you to refine your grammar skills and become a better editor of your own writing. (NOTE: See the Brief Writer's Handbook with Activities, pages 194–198, for additional grammar activities.)

Grammar Topic 3.1

Comparative Forms (-er, more / less; as . . . as, the same . . . as)

There are two ways to form the comparative form of adjectives and adverbs.

1. If the word is one syllable, add -er to the end of the word.

   fast → fast**er**   light → light**er**

   If the word contains two syllables and ends in -y, change the -y to -i and add -er.

   heavy → heav**ier**   lazy → laz**ier**

2. Other words must be preceded by *more* or *less* to form the comparison.

   comfortable → **more** comfortable   quickly → **less** quickly

To say that two things are similar, we use *as . . . as* with adjectives and *the same . . . as* with nouns.

adjective
↓
The concrete block is **as heavy as** the wood block.

noun
↓
The concrete block has **the same weight** as the wood block.

ACTIVITY 10 Working with Comparative Forms

Write the correct comparative form of the word in parentheses.

1. Writing a business letter is (difficult) _____ than composing the same message in an e-mail.

2. I decided not to buy a truck. To me, a car is (reliable) _____ than a truck, but that is just my humble opinion.

3. It did not matter which brand we bought because one is just as (expensive) _____ as the other.

4. Studying physics is a (deep) _____ and more complex process than most people imagine.

5. Most readers prefer the short news clips on Channel 9. It would be impossible to present the news (concisely) _____ than those newscasters do.

6. In the very first lines of the poem, we learn that the main character's jealousy can be attributed to the fact that her younger sister is so much (lucky) _____ than she is.

 For more practice with comparative forms of adjectives and adverbs, try Unit 3, Activity 3 on the *Great Writing 5* Web site: elt.heinle.com/greatwriting

Grammar Topic 3.2

Parallel Comparison

When writers create sentences that contain pairs or a series of items, **parallel construction** in comparison is important. A parallel comparison means that the writer is comparing a noun with a noun or a clause with a clause.

Incorrect:	In general, **a dog's tail** is longer than **a cat.**

This example is wrong because it compares a body part of one animal with another animal in its entirety.

Correction 1:	In general, **a dog's tail** is longer than **a cat's tail.**
Correction 2:	In general, **a dog's tail** is longer than **a cat's.**

Incorrect:	The **smell of fried chicken** is not as strong as **fried fish.**

This is wrong because it compares a smell with a food.

Correction 1:	The **smell of fried chicken** is not as strong as the **smell of fried fish.**
Correction 2:	**Fried chicken** does not smell as strong as **fried fish.**

NOTE: To avoid using the same noun twice, it is common to use the pronouns *that* (singular) or *those* (plural).

Acceptable:	In some countries, the **cost** of water is higher than the **cost** of oil.
Advanced:	In some countries, the **cost** of water is higher than **that** of oil.

ACTIVITY 11 Working with Parallel Comparisons

Each sentence contains an error in parallel comparison. Circle the two items that are being incorrectly compared. Then rewrite the sentence correctly, according to Grammar Topic 3.2. The first one has been done for you.

1. According to the most recent data, the population of Spain is larger than Greece.

   <u>According to the most recent data, the population of Spain is larger than the population of Greece.</u>
   <u>OR According to the most recent data, the population of Spain is larger than that of Greece.</u>

2. The company report indicates that January had more sales than the sales in February.

   _____

   _____

3. With only five days until the deadline, our team's project is not as good as the other team.

   _____

   _____

4. In theory, both classes are equally good. However, last Monday produced a clearly different picture. Professor Smith's students scored better than Professor Beiler.

_____

_____

For more practice with parallel comparisons, try Unit 3, Activity 4 on the *Great Writing 5* Web site: elt.heinle.com/greatwriting

Grammar Topic 3.3
Non-count Nouns

A non-count noun cannot be counted.

Food Items:	butter	sugar	salt	pepper	soup
Liquids:	milk	coffee	water	juice	cream
Academic Subjects:	English	math	science	music	biology
Abstract Ideas:	love	honesty	poverty	crime	advice

NOTE: Count nouns can be counted: *three <u>dogs</u>, two <u>computers</u>, one <u>house</u>, ten <u>motorcycles</u>.*

ACTIVITY 12 Working with Count and Non-count Nouns

Write *many in front of count nouns and make them plural. Write* much *in front of non-count nouns. (They have no plural form.)*

1. _____ pain

2. _____ information

3. _____ decision

4. _____ money

5. _____ pill

6. _____ homework

7. _____ cooperation

8. _____ requirement

Grammar Topic 3.4
Confusing Words: *Than/Then*

The words *than* and *then* sound alike, but they are used very differently. Do not confuse them in your writing.

then = adverb (time)	We are planning to return these books to the library. **Then** we are going to the bank.
than = conjunction	China has more people **than** Brazil does.
= preposition	China has more people **than** cars.

Complete each sentence with than *or* then.

1. If more _____ 50 people come to the meeting, we will need to have it in a larger room.

2. Most supermarkets have express lanes for customers who are purchasing fewer _____ ten items.

3. The rain finally stopped. _____ the players came out onto the field again.

4. If you receive an increase in your salary, _____ you can buy that new furniture.

5. I rode my bike to the grocery store, but _____ I could not find a place to lock it.

Grammar Topic 3.5

Word Parts

You can increase your vocabulary in two basic ways. One way is to learn words that you have never seen before. The second way is to learn word parts, which will help you to understand how other words are constructed. Recognizing word parts and using them correctly will increase your vocabulary and thus improve your writing.

NOTE: See the Brief Writer's Handbook with Activities, pages 192–193, for more information on word parts.

ACTIVITY 14 Editing Word Parts

Read the short story. Five of the eight underlined words contain an error with word parts. Correct the error or write C *(correct). The first one has been done for you.*

EXAMPLE PARAGRAPHS

The Polyglot Parrot

A young man was worried because his grandmother was sad, and

he wondered what he could do to cheer her up. He lived far away, so

he could not be there to keep her company. He decided to send her a

(1.) special _____ C _____ gift—a parrot that

could talk to her so that she would not feel so (2.) loneliness

_____ . When he went to the pet store, he was

(3.) <u>surprising</u> _____ to find a parrot that could speak not one but six languages! This special parrot was (4.) <u>outrageous</u> _____ expensive, but the young man decided that it was worth this extra cost to buy such a wonderful gift for his grandmother. He bought the parrot and sent it to his grandmother's house.

A week later, he called her to see how she and the parrot were (5.) <u>getting</u> _____ along. "Grandmother," he asked, "how did you like my gift?" The grandmother replied, "Well, the parrot was good, but it was a little tough. I should have (6.) <u>cooked</u> _____ it more."

(7.) <u>Shocking</u> _____ beyond belief, the man replied, "What? You ate a parrot that could speak six languages?" The grandmother (8.) <u>quick</u> _____ said, "Well, if the parrot could speak six languages, why didn't it say anything before I put it in the microwave?"

ACTIVITY 15 Review of Grammar Topics 3.1–3.5

Seven of the following ten sentences contain an error involving one of the grammar topics featured in this unit. Write C before the three correct sentences. Write X before the incorrect sentences, circle the error, and write a correction above it.

_____ 1. If this machine could produce more item, our company would buy many more of these machines than we are currently purchasing.

_____ 2. Since the orange juice at this restaurant is more fresher than at the one across the street, I want to eat here.

_____ 3. It is so much more comfortable to spend an evening at home then to go out at night.

_____ 4. My friend Mark took a trip to New Zealand, which he thinks is more fun than a trip to Tasmania.

_____ 5. The Brazilian soccer team's goalie is quicker than Iraq.

_____ 6. Did you get two butters at the store as I requested?

_____ 7. I love my new car; it is more fast and sporty than my last one.

_____ 8. Camping can be a lot of fun, but all of the insects can really annoy me.

_____ 9. There is certainly great poverties in this city.

_____ 10. It is always a great idea to save some of your money for a rainy day, but a lot of people find it difficult not to spend their money immediately.

Seven of the ten underlined words in this paragraph contain an error involving one of the grammar topics featured in this unit. Correct the errors on the lines provided. If the word or phrase is correct, write C.

Comparing Two Books

I read two books on business communication. The first book, *Effective Business Communication*, is an (1.) essential _____ resource on business correspondence for the (2.) modern _____ office. In today's business climate, revolutionized by e-mail and overnight package delivery, it is (3.) increasing _____ important to communicate clearly and (4.) precise _____ in writing. *Effective Business Communication* offers (5.) sound _____ advice for business writers; it is comprehensive yet concise. The second book, *Business Writing for Today*, also claims to be an essential source on business correspondence for today's business world. However, this book is not as well-written or as comprehensive. *Business Writing for Today* discusses a few (6.) aspect _____ of e-mail not covered in *Effective Business Communication*. The authors (7.) than _____ move on to samples of business correspondence, but these samples lack any (8.) informations _____ about the senders' reasons for writing these letters. Therefore, it is my opinion that *Effective Business Communication* would certainly be a (9.) valuabler _____ resource guide to have in the office than (10.) that book _____.

ACTIVITY 17 Word Associations

Circle the word or phrase that is most closely related to the word or phrase on the left. If necessary, use a dictionary to check the meaning of words you do not know.

1. mutts	mixed breeds	pure breeds
2. allergic	to sneeze	to breathe
3. to assume	to believe	to bother
4. stereotypes	emotions	preconceptions
5. aloof	solitary	friendly
6. distant	alone	together
7. finicky	indulgent	picky
8. meticulous	careful	sloppy
9. annoying	helpful	bothersome
10. to frolic	to play	to study
11. neurotically	kindly	crazily
12. ferociously	viciously	sweetly
13. to nip	to bite	to drink
14. an experience	an adventure	a mistake
15. standoffish	haughty	friendly
16. disinterested	aloof	engaged
17. to drop by	to visit	to bomb
18. ridiculously	antagonistically	humorously
19. prejudices	biases	hopes
20. individual	sole	friendly

Fill in each blank with the word or phrase on the left that most naturally completes the phrase on the right. If necessary, use a dictionary to check the meaning of words you do not know.

1. what / that   used to think _____ cold weather was good

2. up / down   growing _____

3. to / of   allergic _____ them

4. up / in   showed _____ at my door

5. about / to   all of the stereotypes _____ pets

6. be / are   supposed to _____

7. belief / news   shocked beyond _____

8. in / on   to frolic _____ the backyard

9. than / then   dogs are friendlier _____ cats

10. in / at   not friendly _____ all

11. ring / punch   to _____ a doorbell

12. around / away   to scare a person _____

13. at / by   dropped _____ her house

14. automobile / answer   a precise _____

15. down / up   to cheer _____ someone

16. on / about   it all depends _____

17. experience / free   after that _____,

18. basic / basis   on the _____ of

19. time / times   at _____

20. expensive / plain   outrageously _____

Original Student Writing: Comparison Essay

In this section, you will follow the seven steps in the writing process to write a comparison essay. To review the details of each step, see Unit 1, pages 7–13.

ACTIVITY 19 Original Comparison Essay

Using the seven steps that follow, write a comparison essay.

Step 1: Choose a Topic

Your first step is to choose a topic for your essay. For a comparison essay, you want to choose a topic for which you can develop three solid points comparing or contrasting the two subjects. Your teacher may assign a topic, you may think of one yourself, or you may choose one from the suggestions below. As you consider possible topics, ask yourself, "What do I know about this topic? What do my readers know? What else do I need to know? Do I need to research this topic?"

Humanities	Comparison essays are quite common in the humanities. If you are a literature major, you might write an essay comparing how two different authors address a similar theme. History majors might compare the ways in which two different leaders responded to similar historical moments. Philosophy majors might compare the relative merits of two systems of thought.
Sciences	Describe a scientific experiment that you performed in which you compared and contrasted two processes. What did you learn from these experiments?
Business	Think of the last major purchase you made (or a major purchase that you will soon make), such as a television, computer, car, or condominium. How did you make your decision? Describe how you compared and contrasted your options. Develop a thesis that reveals how you finally made your decision.
Personal	Who are the two people you most admire? Write an essay describing the influence that these two people have had on your life. You do not have to argue that one was more important than the other.

1. What topic did you choose? _____

2. Why did you choose this topic? _____

_____

_____

3. How well do you know this topic? What is your experience with it?

_____

_____

Step 2: Brainstorm

Use this space to jot down as many ideas about the topic as you can.

Brainstorming Box

Step 3: Outline

Prepare a simple outline of your essay. (This outline is a point-by-point outline, but you may use the block comparison if your teacher approves.)

Title: _____

I. Introduction

   A. Hook: _____

      _____

   B. Connecting information: _____

      _____

      _____

   C. Thesis statement: _____

      _____

II. Body Paragraph 1 (Point of Comparison 1): _____

    A. _____

    B. _____

III. Body Paragraph 2 (Point of Comparison 2): _____

    A. _____

    B. _____

IV. Body Paragraph 3 (Point of Comparison 3): _____

    A. _____

    B. _____

V. Conclusion: _____

_____

Peer Editing of Outlines

Exchange books with a partner. Read your partner's outline. Then use the following questions to help you to comment on your partner's outline. Use your partner's feedback to revise your outline.

1. Is there any aspect of the outline that looks unclear to you?

_____

_____

_____

2. Can you think of an area in the outline that needs more development? Do you have any specific suggestions?

_____

_____

_____

3. If you have any other ideas or suggestions, write them here.

_____

_____

_____

Step 4: Write the First Draft

Use the information from Steps 1, 2, and 3 to write the first draft of your comparison essay. Use at least five of the vocabulary words or phrases presented in Activity 17 and Activity 18. Underline these words and phrases in your essay.

Step 5: Get Feedback from a Peer

Exchange papers from Step 4 with a partner. Read your partner's writing. Then use Peer Editing Sheet 3 on page 213 to help you to comment on your partner's writing. Be sure to offer positive suggestions and comments that will help your partner improve his or her writing.

Step 6: Revise the First Draft

Read the comments on Peer Editing Sheet 3 about your essay. Then reread your essay. Can you identify places where you plan to make revisions? List the improvements you are going to make.

1. _____

_____

_____

2. _____

_____

_____

3. _____

_____

_____

Use all the information from the previous steps to write the final version of your paper. Often, writers will need to write a third or even fourth draft to express their ideas as clearly as possible. Write as many drafts as necessary to produce a good essay.

Step 7: Proofread the Final Draft

Be sure to proofread your paper several times before you submit it.

Additional Topics for Writing

Here are ten topics for additional comparison essay writing.

TOPIC 1: Compare and/or contrast two popular videogame systems. Which videogame system is better and why?

TOPIC 2: Of the two most recent Oscar-winning "Best Pictures," which one do you like better? Why?

TOPIC 3: Compare and/or contrast two of your favorite restaurants.

TOPIC 4: If you were making a movie of your favorite book, who would you cast in the lead role? Compare and/or contrast two actors and discuss which one would be the more appropriate choice.

TOPIC 5:   How did you decide to attend the school you are now attending? Describe the process you used to compare and/or contrast the different schools you considered.

TOPIC 6:   Compare and/or contrast the teaching styles of two of your teachers. Which teaching style is more effective for you? Why?

TOPIC 7:   Compare and/or contrast your hometown to the city you live in now. Which one would you prefer to live in if you had your choice? Why?

TOPIC 8:   Compare and/or contrast your favorite vacation destinations. If you could return to only one for the rest of your life, which would it be? Why?

TOPIC 9:   Look at a local ballot measure in an upcoming election and compare and/or contrast the opposing sides. (Alternatively, you could write about an imaginary election situation.) How would you vote and why?

TOPIC 10:   Compare and/or contrast two sports teams. Which do you think will win the national championship this year? Why?

Timed Writing

How quickly can you write in English? There are many times when you must write quickly, such as on a test. It is important to feel comfortable during those times. Timed-writing practice can make you feel better about writing quickly in English.

First, read the essay guidelines below. Then take out a piece of paper. Read the writing prompt below the guidelines. As quickly as you can, write a basic outline for this writing prompt (including the thesis and your three main points). You should spend <u>no more than</u> 5 minutes on your outline.

You will then have 40 minutes to write a 5-paragraph comparison essay about your topic. At the end of the 40 minutes, your teacher will collect your work and return it to you at a later date.

Comparison Essay Guidelines

- Use the point-by-point method.
- Remember to give your essay a title.
- Double-space your essay.
- Write as legibly as possible (if you are not using a computer).
- Include a short introduction (with a thesis statement), three body paragraphs, and a conclusion.
- Try to give yourself a few minutes before the end of the activity to review your work. Check for spelling, verb tense, and subject-verb agreement mistakes.

> Compare and contrast the values of honor and courage. Which is more important to you? Which is a more important value for your friends to embody? Why?

Cause-Effect Essays | Unit 4

GOAL: To learn how to write a cause-effect essay

*Grammar Topics: 4.1 Maintaining consistent pronouns; 4.2 Sentence fragments; 4.3 Consistent verb tense; 4.4 Confusing words: *it's / its*; 4.5 Word parts

What Is a Cause-Effect Essay?

We all understand cause-effect relationships. For example, if you stay up late the night before a test, hanging out with friends and not studying, you will likely not perform well on the test. A **cause-effect essay** tells how one event (the cause) leads to another event (the effect).

Typically, cause-effect essays work in one of two ways:

- They analyze the ways in which several effects result from a particular cause. ("Focus-on-Effects" Method)
- They analyze the ways in which several causes lead to a particular effect. ("Focus-on-Causes" Method)

Either approach is an effective means of discussing the possible relationship between the two events.

In cause-effect essays, it is easy to suggest that because one event preceded another event, the former event caused the latter. Simply because one event follows another event sequentially does not mean that the two actions are related. For example, people often complain that as soon as they finish washing their car, it starts to rain. Obviously, washing a car does not cause rain. Writers need to be sure that the cause-effect relationship they describe is logical.

How Is a Cause-Effect Essay Organized?

There are two basic ways to organize a cause-effect essay: **focus-on-effects** or **focus-on-causes**.

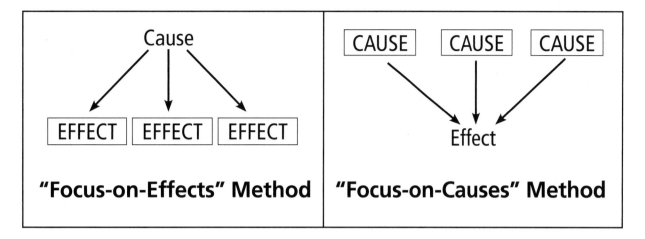

If your assignment is to write a cause-effect essay on the topic of global warming, you could write two kinds of essays:

- In a focus-on-effects essay, you would write about things that are happening as a result of global warming. For example, large parts of the Arctic Circle are melting, thus destroying the habitat of certain wildlife.

- In a focus-on-causes essay, you would write about the causes of global warming, such as excessive carbon dioxide in the atmosphere.

Topics for Cause-Effect Essays

What is a good topic for a cause-effect essay? This type of essay may focus more on the cause or on the effect, but most writers answer this question by thinking of an effect or a final result. The brainstorming stage then includes thinking about one or more causes of that effect.

Here are some possible effects (or results). What might be some causes for each of these effects?

- Pollution is a problem in my country.

- A large percentage of adults cannot read well.

- The rate of violent crime has dropped.

- The voting rate of young adults has recently increased.

- People are saving more of their money than in previous years.

- So-called "extreme sports" are gaining popularity.

ACTIVITY 1 Identifying Topics for Cause-Effect Essays

Read these eight topics. Put a check mark (✔) next to the four that could be good topics for cause-effect essays.

_____ 1. the reasons that a particular candidate won an election

_____ 2. Bangkok versus Singapore as a vacation destination

_____ 3. a trip to visit my grandparents

_____ 4. the increasing use of computers in schools

_____ 5. outlining dietary guidelines for children

_____ 6. how to play the piano

_____ 7. why a student received a scholarship

_____ 8. why life expectancy in many countries is increasing

Think of two additional topics that would be appropriate for a cause-effect essay.

9. _____

10. _____

Supporting Details

After you have selected a topic, your task is to determine whether you will focus more on the causes of the issue or the effects of the issue. This process will also help you to select and develop supporting details for your essay.

ACTIVITY 2 Brainstorming for Two Methods

One of the topics that we hear so much about in today's society is stress. In this activity, you will use the space in the boxes to brainstorm ideas for an essay on the topic of stress. In the first box, your organization will address the focus-on-effects method. In the second box, the method of organization will address the focus-on-causes. Work with other students to complete this activity or discuss your answers with other students after you complete these tasks.

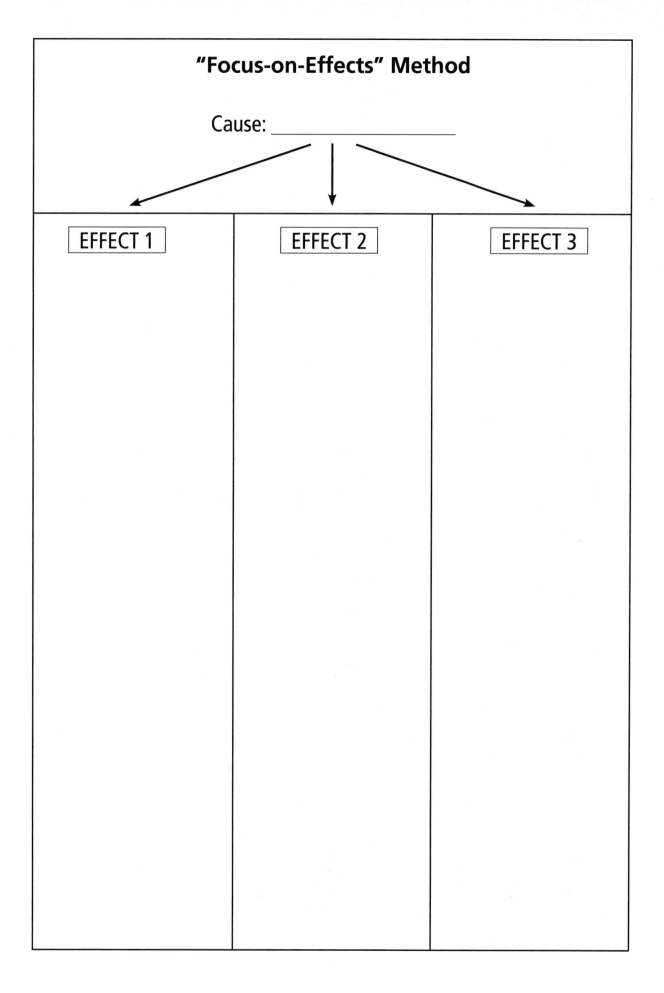

"Focus-on-Effects" Method

Cause: _____

EFFECT 1	EFFECT 2	EFFECT 3

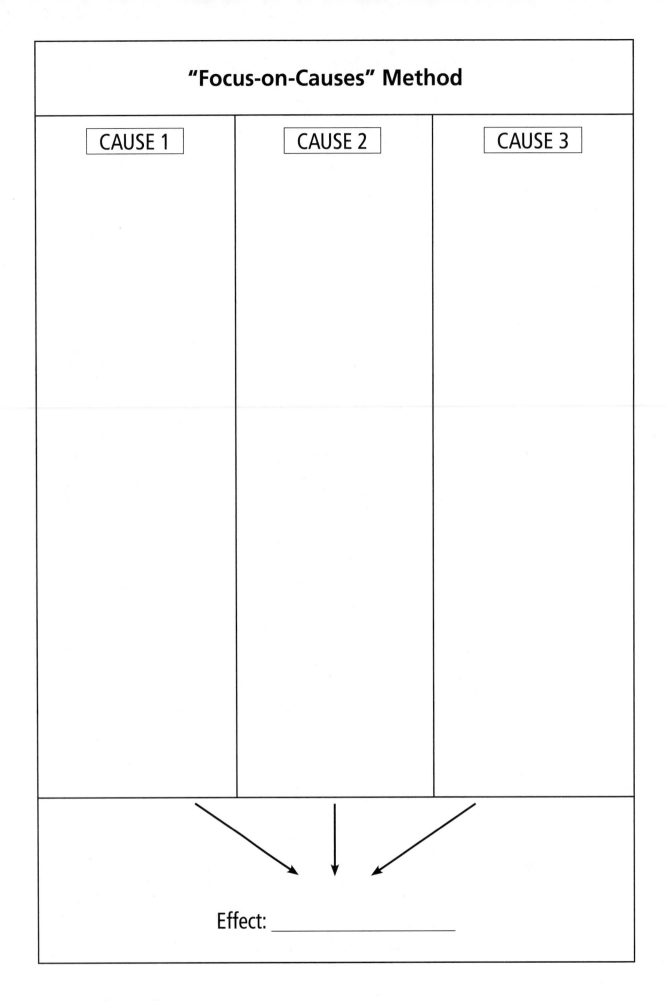

"Focus-on-Causes" Method

CAUSE 1	CAUSE 2	CAUSE 3

Effect: _____

Studying a Sample Cause-Effect Essay

In this section, you will study three versions of a cause-effect essay: a first draft, the same first draft with teacher comments, and the revised essay.

ACTIVITY 3 Warming Up to the Topic

Answer these questions individually. Then discuss them with a partner or in a small group.

1. How often do you listen to music each week? _____ Do you usually listen to music on the radio or to music that you have bought? _____ How many CDs do you own? _____

2. Have you ever made a copy of a music CD? _____ Many people download music from the Internet illegally. Have you or anyone you know ever done this? _____

3. Some people believe that because so many people are downloading music from the Internet, music companies will eventually go bankrupt. Do you think this will happen? _____ Why or why not? _____

   _____

4. Although copying music is illegal, many people continue to download copyrighted materials from the Internet. What are some of the reasons that have caused this practice to be so prevalent?

   _____

   _____

   _____

   _____

   _____

As you read this first draft, look for areas that need improvement.

Music, Computers, and the Recording Industry

The recording industry is in a big hole. Albums and CDs are not selling as much as several years ago, and this **trend** shows no sign of reversing. For the industry as a whole, profits are down ten percent inside the last three year. What has caused this downward **spiral** for the music industry? The answer is an equipment with which I am writing this essay: the personal computer. There are three reasons that the computer has had a bad effect in the recording industry.

Due to it is popular to share computer sound files, consumers no longer feel that they are need to purchase music. Many people think it is **morally** acceptable—not to mention convenience—to download music files for free via file-sharing services. A couple of mouse-button click, and **presto**! Now you "own" on your own computer that nice little tune that you have been **humming.** Then it was just a couple of more clicks until it was burned on a CD for you. With this level of convenience, it was easy to see why record companies are **feeling the pinch.**

Computers allow music people to **market** and sell their own music. Music people can record and create their own CDs at a relatively **modest** cost these days. Before the development of the personal computer, this would have been impossibility. For this reason, it makes less sense for music people to give away a part of their profits to a record company for activities that he can accomplish themselves.

The recording industry bears some of the blame for its own problems. Simply because they have been shy about using personal computers to sell its products. It has long annoy me that record companies primarily sell albums when all I want is one song. Too many albums contained only one good song, and I do not like to spend money for an entire album when I wanted only one song. The recording industry should package and sell music in a way that consumers want. And take advantage of personal computers to market songs to individual consumers.

If the downward trends in the recording industry continues, there will still be a recording industry? It is quite possible that the recording industry will stop over time if it becomes no longer profitable for them to market and sell music. Performing artists have to advertise themselves through smaller **venues,** and consumers might need to seek out new music if its no longer marketed directly to us. The computer will **bring about** tremendous changes to the recording industry. The industry will have to move quickly to **retain** its **relevance** in the today's economy.

a trend: a new style that people follow
a spiral: a winding curve that moves toward a fixed center
morally: ethically, honorably
presto: an expression that indicates something has been accomplished instantly
hum: to sing without words
feel the pinch: to suffer the consequences

market: to sell or offer something for sale
modest: moderate in amount
a venue: a location
bring about: to cause to happen
retain: to keep possession of something
relevance: importance in relation to the matter being considered

Read the teacher comments on the first draft of "Music, Computers, and the Recording Industry." Are these the same things that you noticed?

Your title is not very catchy, but it works OK.

ESSAY 4B

Music, Computers, and the Recording Industry

vague vocab

The recording industry is in a big hole. Albums and CDs are not selling as much

they were (You need parallel comparison.)

as several years ago, and this trend shows no sign of reversing. For the industry as a whole,

word choice

profits are down ten percent inside the last three year. What has caused this downward spiral

non-count noun

for the music industry? The answer is an equipment with which I am writing this essay: the

prep.

personal computer. There are three reasons that the computer has had a bad effect in the

recording industry.

word choice: BAD is a beginning word. How about DELETERIOUS?

"Due to" is followed by a noun, not a sentence

Due to it is popular to share computer sound files, consumers no longer feel that they

are need to purchase music. Many people think it is morally acceptable—not to mention

?

convenience—to download music files for free via file-sharing services. A couple of

use a more specific word

mouse-button clicks, and presto! Now you "own" on your own computer that nice little tune

that you have been humming. Then it was just a couple of more clicks until it was burned

on a CD for you. With this level of convenience, it was easy to see why record companies are

Why change to past tense?

feeling the pinch.

Transition?   *vocab?*

Computers allow music people to market and sell their own music. Music people

can record and create their own CDs at a relatively modest cost these days. Before the

word form

development of the personal computer, this would have been impossibility. For this reason,

it makes less sense for music people to give away a part of their profits to a record company

for activities that he can accomplish themselves.

Pronouns: be consistent with singular and plural

Transition?

The recording industry bears some of the blame for its own problems. Simply because

wrong word—people are shy, not companies—What do you mean?

verb form   fragment

they have been shy about using personal computers to sell its products. It has long annoy me

good adverb

that record companies primarily sell albums when all I want is one song. Too many albums contained only one good song, and I do not like to spend money for an entire album when

Why change to past tense?

I wanted only one song. The recording industry should package and sell music in a way

that consumers want. And take advantage of personal computers to market songs to

individual consumers. *fragment*

If the downward trends in the recording industry continues, there will still be a recording

industry? *word choice: die?* It is quite possible that the recording industry will stop over time if it becomes

no longer profitable ~~for them~~ to market and sell music. Performing artists have to advertise

Parallel? Repeat modal "might" *word form*

themselves through smaller venues, and consumers might need to seek out new music if its

Pronoun?

no longer marketed directly to us. The computer will bring about tremendous changes to

connect *here, future is correct*

the recording industry. The industry will have to move quickly to retain its relevance in the

Excellent word combinations!

today's economy.

Your ideas flow really well in this essay. I sense that you feel strongly about this issue.

I especially liked your vocabulary choices in the last paragraph.

Paragraphs 3 and 4 need transitions. Do you see that your opening sentences sound rather abrupt?

Read the revised version of the essay, now titled "Modern Music Technology: Downloading or Stealing?" What has been changed? What still needs improvement?

ESSAY 4C

Modern Music Technology: Downloading or Stealing?

The recording industry is in a **slump**. Albums and CDs are not selling as much as they were several years ago, and this trend shows no sign of reversing. For the industry as a whole, profits are down ten percent within the last three years. What has caused this downward spiral for the music industry? The answer is the same piece of equipment with which I am writing this essay: the personal computer. There are three reasons that the computer has had a **deleterious** effect on the recording industry.

Because of the popularity of sharing computer sound files, consumers no longer feel that they need to purchase music. Many people think it is morally acceptable—not to mention convenient—to download music files for free via file-sharing services. A couple of mouse-button clicks, and presto! Now you "own" on your own computer that **catchy** little tune that you have been humming. Then it is just a couple of more clicks until it is burned on a CD for you. With this level of convenience, it is easy to see why record companies are feeling the pinch.

In addition, computers allow musicians to market and sell their own music. Musicians can record and create their own CDs at a relatively modest cost these days. Before the development of the personal computer, most musicians could not afford to record their own music, but now the costs are much more reasonable. For this reason, it makes less sense for musicians to give away a part of their profits to a record company for activities that they can accomplish themselves.

Furthermore, the recording industry bears some of the blame for its own problems simply because it has been **recalcitrant** about using personal computers to sell its products.

It has long annoyed me that record companies primarily sell whole albums when only one of the songs is of interest to me. I do not like to waste my money on an entire album and then find out that the album has just one good song on it. The recording industry should package and sell music in a way that consumers want and take advantage of personal computers to market songs to individual consumers.

If the downward trends in the recording industry continue, will there still be a recording industry? It is quite possible that the recording industry will die over time if it becomes no longer profitable to market and sell music. Performing artists might have to advertise themselves through smaller venues, and consumers might need to seek out new music if it is no longer marketed directly to them. The computer has brought about tremendous changes to the recording industry, and the industry will have to move quickly to retain its relevance in today's economy.

a slump: a sudden decline
deleterious: harmful

catchy: attractive or appealing
recalcitrant: not willing, stubborn

Analyzing Content and Organization

ACTIVITY 7 Analyzing the Content

Answer these questions about the revised version (Essay 4C) of "Modern Music Technology: Downloading or Stealing?"

1. What is the topic? _____

2. Write the thesis statement here: _____

   _____

3. What is the effect that the writer describes in the essay?

   _____

   _____

4. What are some of the causes that the writer describes?

   _____

   _____

5. Is the writer's reasoning convincing? _____

   How could it be improved? _____

   _____

ACTIVITY 8 Analyzing the Organization

Read the outline of "Modern Music Technology: Downloading or Stealing?" Then use information in the box to complete the outline.

> - a decrease in sales of CDs and albums
> - current conditions
> - the recording industry
> - personal computer
> - musicians

I. Introduction

   A. Describe the current troubled situation of the recording industry.

   B. Thesis statement: The _____ has caused many

      of the recording industry's woes.

II. Body Paragraph 1: Show that the popularity of sharing computer files has led to _____

_____

III. Body Paragraph 2: Describe how computers allow _____

to market their own music without the recording industry.

IV. Body Paragraph 3: Suggest that _____ bears some

responsibility because it has not marketed through personal computers.

V. Conclusion

  A. Ponder the future of the recording industry if _____ remain.

  B. Suggest that the recording industry must act quickly to reverse these declines.

Writer's Note

Language for Conversation and for Writing

Language in conversation, especially between people who know each other well, is usually informal. Language in writing, in contrast, is often more formal. Language in writing has a different style than language in conversation. We use different vocabulary and sometimes different structures for conversation and for writing.

Here are some examples of differences in these two language styles.

Conversation	Writing
kids	children
a cool movie	a great movie, a really interesting movie
See you later!	I hope to see you soon.
Well, this is the reason . . .	The reason is . . .

Can you think of other pairs that are more appropriate for conversation or for writing?

Building Better Sentences

Correct and varied sentence structure is essential to the quality of your writing. For further practice with "Modern Music Technology: Downloading or Stealing?" go to Practice 4 on page 205 in Appendix 1.

Transitions and Connectors in Cause-Effect Essays

The most commonly used transitions and connectors in cause-effect essays are words or phrases that indicate causation or effect. Perhaps the most familiar cause-effect transition word is *because*: "X happened because Y happened."

Transitions and Connectors Commonly Used in Cause-Effect Essays		
(X can be) attributed to (Y)	(the) effect (of X)	(X is the) reason for (Y)
because	(a key) factor of (X)	(X is a) reflection of (Y)
because of	furthermore	(as a) result
(X is the) cause of (Y)	if / if (X), then (Y)	(X) resulted in (Y)
(X is) caused by (Y)	in addition (to)	since
(as a) consequence	(X) leads to (Y)	so
(one) consequence of this (is that . . .)	on account of	therefore
consequently	owing to	this means that . . .
due to	(for this) reason	thus

ACTIVITY 9 Using Transitions and Connectors

Reread the revised version (Essay 4C) of "Modern Music Technology: Downloading or Stealing?" on pages 92–93. Find and list six transitions or connectors and write the paragraph number after each. The first one has been done for you.

1. _____ *because of* _____ (2)

2. _____ (   )

3. _____ (   )

4. _____ (   )

5. _____ (   )

6. _____ (   )

 For more practice with structure of cause-effect essays, try Unit 4, Activity 1 on the *Great Writing 5* Web site: elt.heinle.com/greatwriting

This section will help you to refine your grammar skills and become a better editor of your own writing. (NOTE: See the Brief Writer's Handbook with Activities, pages 194–198, for additional grammar activities.)

Grammar Topic 4.1

Maintaining Consistent Pronouns

Good writers consistently use pronouns of the first, second, or third person throughout an essay: first person (*I, we*), second person (*you*), or third person (*he, she, it, they*).

Incorrect:	When **students** have a major exam, **you** should begin preparing early.
Correct:	When **students** have a major exam, **they** should begin preparing early.
Incorrect:	In the story, **you** can see that the young girl is going to be successful. **We** know this because of her determination and cleverness.
Correct:	In the story, **we** can see that the young girl is going to be successful. **We** know this because of her determination and cleverness.

ACTIVITY 10 Working with Pronoun Consistency

Make the pronouns consistent in each sentence.

1. It was raining. You could see people running for cover under trees, under awnings, under anything that offered protection. We thought the rain would stop soon.

2. If one studies, you will do well on the quizzes.

3. In the novel I am reading, we find it difficult to trust certain characters. You cannot easily explain why, but we have that reaction to them.

4. If I consider her last short story, then we can definitely say that this writer's attitude toward immigration is changing.

 For more practice with consistent pronoun use, try Unit 4, Activity 2 on the *Great Writing 5* Web site: elt.heinle.com/greatwriting

Grammar Topic 4.2

Sentence Fragments

For many writers, sentence fragments, or incomplete sentences, are difficult to avoid. Because fragments are one of the most serious errors, it is imperative to learn how to recognize and correct them.

Fragment:	I scored 97 on the quiz. **Because I read and studied the textbook often.**
Correction:	I scored 97 on the quiz **because I read and studied the textbook often.**
Fragment:	The postcard was filled with natural beauty. **The red of the sunset, the brilliance of the sand, and the sparkle in the water.**
Correction:	The postcard was filled with natural beauty, **such as the red of the sunset, the brilliance of the sand, and the sparkle in the water.**

NOTE: See the Brief Writer's Handbook with Activities, pages 184–190, for more work with fragments and sentence variety.

ACTIVITY 11 Working with Fragments

Write C *on the line next to complete sentences. Write* F *if there is a fragment and circle the fragment.*

_____ 1. Despite the heavy wind and the torrential rain, the young trees around the lake were able to survive the bad weather. It was a miracle.

_____ 2. The huge, two-story houses all have a very similar design. With no difference except the color of the roofs.

_____ 3. Ireland has a rich and colorful history. One with many stories of fairies and elves.

_____ 4. Shopping malls are a very popular tourist attraction in many cities, but some tourists are not interested in them. Shopping is not for everyone.

_____ 5. Because of the popularity of the film. Producers were anxious to begin work on its sequel.

_____ 6. The chef added so much spice to the stew that only the most daring of his patrons tasted it. The result was that less than half of the food was consumed.

_____ 7. There was a strange tension in the air. After so many years of separation.

_____ 8. My mother is so organized that she uses a color-coding system in her kitchen pantry. My father, on the other hand, is one of the most unorganized people I know.

_____ 9. What is a dream and why do we dream? Scientists really do not understand dreams, but I wish someone could explain them to me.

_____ 10. Thousands of commuters were late for work this morning. Since the bus workers are on strike over pay and health benefits.

For more practice with sentence fragments, try Unit 4, Activity 3 on the *Great Writing 5* Web site: elt.heinle.com/greatwriting

Grammar Topic 4.3
Consistent Verb Tense

Good writers are careful to use the same verb tense throughout an essay. If you are writing about an event that happened in the past, keep all the verbs in one or more of the past tenses (simple past, past progressive, past perfect, past perfect progressive). Likewise, if you are describing an event in the present, maintain one or more of the present tenses throughout. Do not change verb tenses without a specific reason.

ACTIVITY 12 Working with Consistent Verb Tense

Circle the verbs where the tense shifts for no reason.

EXAMPLE PARAGRAPH

Ethics in Making a Good Speech

A good presentation can have significant and long-lasting effects on an audience. What happens between speakers and their presentation and the audience involved many factors. Like any tool, a presentation can be applied with skill to achieve a useful purpose, or it can be used to damage and destroy. Although a hammer was used to build a home, it also can be used to punch holes in a wall. One unethical presentation can affect the way that an audience sees you in all future encounters. Thus, we believed that a good speaker must ask and answer important ethical questions at every point in the speech-making process. Ethical decision making was more than a means of improving speaker credibility; it will remain a moral obligation of every good speaker.

Grammar Topic 4.4
Confusing Words: *It's / Its*

The words *it's* and *its* sound alike, but they are used very differently. Do not confuse them in your writing.

it's = contraction (*it is*) Are you sure that **it's (it is)** really after midnight?

its = possessive adjective The cat will clean **its** fur before going to sleep.

NOTE 1: A common error is to use *its'* with an apostrophe at the end. Remember that *its'* is not a word.

NOTE 2: Contractions are used primarily in informal writing such as e-mails and dialogs.

ACTIVITY 13 Working with Confusing Words: *It's / Its*

Complete each sentence with its *or* it's.

1. The company released _____ report on Tuesday; _____ full of very good economic indicators.

2. The cat purred when the kind lady rubbed _____ fur.

3. Whose key chain is this? If _____ Susan's, then I will call her to tell her that _____ here. If _____ Will's, I cannot let him know that _____ here because I do not have his cell phone or his home number. I would look up his home number in the phone directory, but I believe _____ unlisted.

4. Sometimes a dog's bark is worse than _____ bite; this fact is the basis for a common proverb.

Grammar Topic 4.5
Word Parts

You can increase your vocabulary in two basic ways. One way is to learn words that you have never seen before. The second way is to learn word parts, which will help you to understand how other words are constructed. Recognizing word parts and using them correctly will increase your vocabulary and thus improve your writing.

NOTE: See the Brief Writer's Handbook with Activities, pages 192–193, for more information on word parts.

Read the following paragraph. Five of the eight underlined words contain an error with word parts. Correct the error or write C (correct).

Political Parties in the United States

In every U.S. (1.) <u>president</u> _____ election since 1952, voters across

the nation have been asked, "(2.) <u>General</u> _____ speaking, do you think of

yourself as a Republican, a Democrat, an (3.) <u>Independent</u> _____, or what?"

Most voters think of themselves as either Republicans or Democrats, but the (4.) <u>proportion</u>

_____ of those who think of themselves as Independents has increased

over time. The size of the Democratic Party's (5.) <u>major</u> _____ has also

shrunk. Nevertheless, most (6.) <u>America</u> _____ today still (7.) <u>identification</u>

_____ with one of these two major parties, and Democrats still outnumber

Republicans. The question on many (8.) <u>politicians'</u> _____ minds is whether

this situation will continue or not.

ACTIVITY 15 Review of Grammar Topics 4.1–4.5

Seven of the following ten sentences contain an error involving one of the grammar topics featured in this unit. Write C before the three correct sentences. Write X before the incorrect sentences, circle the error, and write a correction above it.

_____ 1. When the schoolchildren visited the museum, their teacher advised him to be quiet.

_____ 2. I cannot wait to go to work today. Because I think I am going to get a raise!

_____ 3. Sylvia played softball when she was younger, and she always hits home runs then.

_____ 4. It's good for them to have an extra turn, but is it good for us?

_____ 5. Its not healthy to eat only foods with a lot of sugar.

_____ 6. The marching band, entering with a great roar of music.

_____ 7. Simon argued that the judge was incompetent in the trial and that a mistrial should be declared.

_____ 8. The car needs a new paint job since it's trunk is getting rusty.

_____ 9. Akio knew the truth, but she was afraid to tell the police.

_____ 10. Due to the large influx of immigrants into Canada beginning in the 1950s.

For more practice with the grammar topics from this unit, try Unit 4, Activity 4 on the *Great Writing 5* Web site: elt.heinle.com/greatwriting

ACTIVITY 16 Editing a Paragraph: Review of Grammar Topics 4.1–4.5

Seven of the ten underlined portions in the following paragraph contain an error involving one of the grammar topics featured in this unit. Correct the errors on the lines provided. If the word or phrase is correct, write C.

EXAMPLE PARAGRAPH

The Impact of E-mail on Communication

(1.) <u>On</u> _____ e-mail, messages are composed, transmitted, and usually read on computer (2.) <u>screens. Today</u> _____ e-mail has replaced the (3.) <u>telephone. As</u> _____ the preferred medium to communicate in business. In 1997, for the first time ever, more e-mail was sent than letters via the post office. In a recent American Management Association (4.) <u>surveying,</u> _____ 36 percent of executives reported that (5.) <u>you</u> _____ favor e-mail for most management (6.) <u>communicate,</u> _____ compared with 26 percent who preferred the phone. Surprisingly, one of the less (7.) <u>popular</u> _____ alternatives was a face-to-face meeting, favored by only 15 percent of the (8.) <u>executives. One</u> _____ executive said, "(9.) <u>Its</u> _____ only a matter of time before we do away with face-to-face business deals (10.) <u>complete</u> _____."

ACTIVITY 17 Word Associations

Circle the word or phrase that is most closely related to the word or phrase on the left. If necessary, use a dictionary to check the meaning of words you do not know.

1. to hum	a song	a file
2. a slump	a high point	a low point
3. a trend	moderate	pattern
4. reversing	going backward	going forward
5. profits	more money	less money
6. spiral	twists and turns	a straight road
7. deleterious	positive	negative
8. morally	good behavior	crime
9. to retain	to keep	to clean
10. via	about	through
11. presto	immediately	after a long effort
12. feeling the pinch	in a bind	free to go
13. to market	to sell	to reverse
14. modest	reasonable	exorbitant
15. an impossibility	likely	unlikely
16. activities	decisions	events
17. recalcitrant	anxious	stubborn
18. tremendous	little	big
19. industry	natural resources	business
20. relevance	importance	unimportance

ACTIVITY 18 Using Collocations

Fill in each blank with the word or phrase on the left that most naturally completes the phrase on the right. If necessary, use a dictionary to check the meaning of words you do not know.

1. in / on   to be _____ a slump

2. future / ago   several years _____

3. in / of   no sign _____ reversing

4. on / as   _____ a whole

5. within / ago   _____ the last three years

6. about / on   to have an effect _____ the economy

7. of / about   due to the popularity _____

8. at / to   they need _____ purchase

9. via / around   to get data _____ file-sharing services

10. on / in   to have a program _____ your computer

11. of / in   a couple _____ more clicks

12. at / from   _____ a relatively modest cost

13. away / from   to give _____ a part

14. of / on   to bear some _____ the blame

15. about / on   to be recalcitrant _____

16. in / of   its relevance _____ today's economy

17. many / much   to know so _____ about a topic

18. about / over   will die _____ time

19. up / out   to seek _____

20. to / with   if it is no longer marketed directly _____ the public

Original Student Writing: Cause-Effect Essay

In this section, you will follow the seven steps in the writing process to write a cause-effect essay. To review the details of each step, see Unit 1, pages 7–13.

ACTIVITY 19 Original Cause-Effect Essay

Using the seven steps that follow, write a cause-effect essay.

Step 1: Choose a Topic

Your first step is to choose a topic for your essay. Choose a topic that you understand well, including the causes and effects of the topic. Your teacher may assign a topic, you may think of one yourself, or you may choose one from the suggestions below. As you consider possible topics, ask yourself, "What do I know about this topic? What do my readers know? Even though I know this topic well, is there additional information that I need in order to explain the topic better to my readers?"

Humanities	Cause-effect essays are very popular in history courses. Choose a famous historical event and explain what the causes of this event were.
Sciences	Virtually all scientific experiments describe cause-effect relationships. Write an essay in which you describe a laboratory experiment that allows you to draw conclusions about the causes of a certain event.
Business	All businesses desire the same effect: to sell more of their product. Develop a business model that explains how adopting certain marketing strategies will increase sales.
Personal	What were the reasons that you decided to attend the college you decided to attend? Write an essay that articulates the reasons (the causes) for your decision about which school to attend (the effect).

1. What topic did you choose? _____

2. Why did you choose this topic? _____

   _____

   _____

3. How well do you know this topic? What is your experience with it?

   _____

   _____

Step 2: Brainstorm

Use this space to jot down as many ideas about the topic as you can.

Brainstorming Box

Step 3: Outline

Prepare a simple outline of your essay. Decide whether you will use the focus-on-causes method or the focus-on-effects method. Refer to the diagrams on pages 83–86.

Title: _____

Type of cause-effect essay (*circle one*):   focus-on-causes   focus-on-effects

  I. Introduction

    A. Hook: _____

_____

B. Connecting information: _____

_____

_____

C. Thesis statement: _____

_____

II. Body Paragraph 1 (Cause/Effect 1): _____

   A. _____

   B. _____

III. Body Paragraph 2 (Cause/Effect 2): _____

   A. _____

   B. _____

IV. Body Paragraph 3 (Cause/Effect 3): _____

   A. _____

   B. _____

V. Conclusion: _____

_____

Peer Editing of Outlines

Exchange books with a partner. Read your partner's outline. Then use the following questions to help you to comment on your partner's outline. Use your partner's feedback to revise your outline.

1. Is there any aspect of the outline that looks unclear to you?

_____

_____

_____

2. Can you think of an area in the outline that needs more development? Do you have any specific suggestions?

_____

_____

_____

_____

Step 4: Write the First Draft

Use the information from Steps 1, 2, and 3 to write the first draft of your cause-effect essay. Use at least five of the vocabulary words or phrases presented in Activity 17 and Activity 18. Underline these words and phrases in your essay.

Step 5: Get Feedback from a Peer

Exchange papers from Step 4 with a partner. Read your partner's writing. Then use Peer Editing Sheet 4 on page 215 to help you to comment on your partner's writing. Be sure to offer positive suggestions and comments that will help your partner improve his or her writing.

Step 6: Revise the First Draft

Read the comments on Peer Editing Sheet 4 about your essay. Then reread your essay. Can you identify places where you plan to make revisions? List the improvements you are going to make.

1. _____

_____

_____

2. _____

_____

_____

3. _____

_____

_____

Use all the information from the previous steps to write the final version of your paper. Often, writers will need to write a third or even fourth draft to express their ideas as clearly as possible. Write as many drafts as necessary to produce a good essay.

Step 7: Proofread the Final Draft

Be sure to proofread your paper several times before you submit it.

Additional Topics for Writing

Here are ten topics for additional cause-effect essay writing.

TOPIC 1:   What are the effects of beauty or good looks?

TOPIC 2:   What are the causes of illiteracy?

TOPIC 3:   What are the effects of obesity?

TOPIC 4:   What are the effects of overcrowding, either in a university dormitory or in a city?

TOPIC 5:   Discuss how people's childhood experiences influence their lives.

TOPIC 6:   What effect can one person have on the government?

TOPIC 7:   What are the effects of sudden wealth (such as when a person wins the lottery)?

TOPIC 8:   What are the effects of poverty?

TOPIC 9:   What are the causes of happiness?

TOPIC 10: What are the causes of a recent political crisis?

Timed Writing

How quickly can you write in English? There are many times when you must write quickly, such as on a test. It is important to feel comfortable during those times. Timed-writing practice can make you feel better about writing quickly in English.

First, read the essay guidelines below. Then take out a piece of paper. Read the writing prompt below the guidelines. As quickly as you can, write a basic outline for this writing prompt (including the thesis and your three main points). You should spend <u>no more than</u> 5 minutes on your outline.

You will then have 40 minutes to write a 5-paragraph cause-effect essay about your topic. At the end of the 40 minutes, your teacher will collect your work and return it to you at a later date.

Cause-Effect Essay Guidelines

- Decide which method is best for the topic: focus-on-effects or focus-on-causes.

- Remember to give your essay a title.

- Double-space your essay.

- Write as legibly as possible (if you are not using a computer).

- Include a short introduction (with a thesis statement), three body paragraphs, and a conclusion.

- Try to give yourself a few minutes before the end of the activity to review your work. Check for spelling, verb tense, and subject-verb agreement mistakes.

> We all face personal troubles in our lives. Think about a recent challenging situation in your life at home, at work, at school, or with friends. What were the causes of this situation? What were its effects? How did you resolve this situation?

Argumentative Essays

GOAL: To learn how to write an argumentative essay

***Grammar Topics:** 5.1 Preposition combinations; 5.2 Verb tense with *if* in future time; 5.3 *Because* and *because of*; 5.4 Confusing words: *to/too/two*; 5.5 Word parts

What Is an Argumentative Essay?

We frequently attempt to persuade our friends to agree with our viewpoints, whether the subject is which movie to watch or where to go on vacation. In writing an **argumentative essay**, we use written words to achieve a similar goal. In argumentative essays, sometimes referred to as persuasive essays, writers attempt to convince their readers to agree with them on a particular issue. By explaining their reasons for holding a particular belief, writers share their perceptions of an issue and hope to sway others to share their point of view.

Perhaps the most common type of argumentative essay is the newspaper editorial.* In newspaper editorials, writers choose an issue and explain its relevance to their readers. By educating their readers on a given topic, the writers hope to create a community of like-minded thinkers. For example, editorial writers often endorse particular candidates in elections; they want to persuade their readers to vote for the candidates who the writers think will do the best job.

At their best, argumentative essays clearly and logically explain a writer's reasons behind a given viewpoint. However, writers should not exaggerate their claims. It is better to be candid about the limitations of your viewpoint than to overstate the case.

How Is an Argumentative Essay Organized?

An argumentative essay is organized in the same general manner as the other essays we have studied in this book.

- It begins with an **introductory paragraph** in which the writer introduces the topic and thesis of the essay.

- The **body paragraphs** discuss the pros and cons of the thesis statement. It is logical for all essay types to have supporting information in the body paragraphs, but an argumentative essay often contains a counterargument, which is an opposing opinion, in the body of the essay. This counterargument is presented, explained, and then shown to be insufficient. In other words, you present an argument against your opinion, and then you refute it.

*We strongly recommend reading an editorial in a newspaper of your choice to help you understand what argumentative writing is. In fact, you should read editorials in three different newspapers or similar sources to become familiar with the writing style and organization of good argumentative writing.

One way to organize the body paragraphs is for the first body paragraph to address the benefits of the writer's position on an issue and the second body paragraph to introduce a counterargument and then address its limitations. The third body paragraph might offer a compromise between the writer's position and the opposing point of view.

Another way to organize the body paragraphs is for Paragraphs 2 and 3 to provide support for your essay and then for Paragraph 4 to introduce and then refute your counterargument.

- The **conclusion** summarizes the state of the issue and restates the writer's thesis.

Writer's Note

All Essays Are Argumentative Writing

All of the essay types in this book—process analysis, comparison, cause-effect, argumentative, and narrative—can be seen as argumentative essays. A process analysis essay attempts to persuade the reader that the process being described is the most appropriate means of achieving a desired result. Comparison essays and cause-effect essays likewise persuade the reader that the writer's thesis is the correct way of analyzing a given situation. When you write a narrative essay, you are convincing readers to see some aspect of your life in a certain way. When you write in any rhetorical mode, persuasion is always one of your goals. You want your reader to share your view of the world around you.

Topics for Argumentative Essays

What is a good topic for an argumentative essay? Obviously, it should be an issue that you feel strongly about and would like to share your opinions on. What is your opinion on the issue? Why do you feel this way? Can you think of some reasons that people might think differently than you do?

Here are some general topics that lend themselves well to an argumentative essay:

- limiting oil exploration in environmentally sensitive areas
- capital punishment
- mandatory military service
- raising the driving age
- merits of standardized testing
- using animals for medical research

ACTIVITY 1 Identifying Topics for Argumentative Essays

Read these eight topics. Put a check mark (✔) next to the four that could be good topics for argumentative essays.

_____ 1. the first time I flew in a plane

_____ 2. whom to vote for in an upcoming election

_____ 3. how and why birds migrate south for the winter

_____ 4. steps in negotiating an international contract

_____ 5. the necessity of higher taxes on gasoline

_____ 6. why schools should offer after-school programs for at-risk students

_____ 7. reasons that you deserve a raise at your job

_____ 8. how to play chess

Think of two additional topics that would be appropriate for an argumentative essay.

9. _____

10. _____

Supporting Details

After you have selected a topic, you will need to think about what you already know about the issue and what you need to find out. Asking yourself questions about both sides of the issue is a good way to generate details to include in your essay.

ACTIVITY 2 Brainstorming Supporting Ideas

Read the following thesis statements. What are three ideas to support it? Can you think of three ideas against it?

1. *Thesis statement:* Adults should be required to pass a test before they can be parents.

   Supporting ideas:

   a. _____

   b. _____

   c. _____

   Opposing ideas:

   a. _____

   b. _____

   c. _____

2. *Thesis statement:* The death penalty helps society to protect innocent people.

   Supporting ideas:

   a. _____

   b. _____

   c. _____

   Opposing ideas:

   a. _____

   b. _____

   c. _____

Studying a Sample Argumentative Essay

In this section, you will study three versions of an argumentative essay: a first draft, the same first draft with teacher comments, and the revised essay.

ACTIVITY 3 Warming Up to the Topic

Answer these questions individually. Then discuss them with a partner or in a small group.

1. How many e-mail accounts do you currently have? _____

2. How often do you check your e-mail? _____

3. About how many e-mails do you receive each day? How many of these e-mail messages are spam?

   _____

4. Some people are so annoyed by spam that they want laws to punish spammers. Do you agree or

   disagree with this idea? _____

   Why or why not? Give two reasons.

   a. _____

   _____

   _____

   _____

   b. _____

   _____

   _____

   _____

As you read this first draft, look for areas that need improvement.

ESSAY 5A

<u>Can</u> Spam!

When I first got an e-mail account ten years ago, I received communications only from friends, family, and professional **acquaintances**. Businesses do not contact to me with advertisements to sell me their services. Now it seems that every time I check my e-mail, I have to delete a lot of advertisements and other correspondence. I have no interest in reading this. If we want e-mail to continue to be useful. We need laws that make criminal spam. The **avalanche** of spam threaten to destroy this important means in communication.

If the government will not do something soon to outlaw spam, the problem will get much more bad. Computer programs allow spammers sending hundreds of millions of e-mails virtually instantly. As more and more advertisers turn to spam to sell their products, the e-mail that we want to receive it could be greatly outnumbered for junk e-mail. Would you continue to use e-mail if you had to delete 100 pieces spam for each e-mail that was written to you by someone you know?

Companies rely with e-mail for their employees to communicate with each other. Spamming corrupts their internal communications, and they are unable to communicate effectively. Such a situation results with a lost of productivity for the company and requires sometimes the company to reformulate its communication network, to.

Despite of these problems for businesses, some people might discuss that criminalizing spam would infringe on spammers' right to free speech. However, how free is speech that drowns out another voices that we want to hear? The right to free speech does not allow companies to flood my mail box with its e-mail garbage. Yes, free speech is an **essential** component of the exchange with ideas necessary for **flourishing** democracy. Unsolicited e-mails, however, threaten to inhibit effective communication, not nurture it.

Because these reasons, our lawmakers need to legislate against spam. Spammers should be fined, and perhaps jailed, if they continue to disturb people with their **incessant** pleas of our attention and our money. E-mail was designed for be a helpful tool for allow people all over the world too communicate with each other quick and effective, but spam threatens to destroy this advance in the human communication.

can: to throw away, eliminate
an acquaintance: a person whom one knows but who is not a close friend
an avalanche: a massive or overwhelming amount

essential: necessary
flourishing: thriving, healthy
incessant: constant

Read the teacher comments on the first draft of "Can Spam!" Are these the same things that you noticed?

ESSAY 5B

The command in the title
really grabs our attention

Can Spam!

When I first got an e-mail account ten years ago, I received communications

only from friends, family, and professional acquaintances. Businesses (do) not

prep.
contact (to) me with advertisements to sell me their services. Now it seems that

use a more advanced word
every time I check my e-mail, I have to delete (a lot of) advertisements and other

combine (embed)
correspondence. I have no interest in reading this. If we want e-mail to continue to

good vocab!
be useful. We need laws that (make criminal) spam. The avalanche of spam threaten

prep.   See how this phrase is so much
to destroy this important means (in) communication.   better than the boring "a lot of"?

verb tense after "if"?
If the government will not do something soon to outlaw spam, the problem

will get much (more bad.) Computer programs allow spammers (sending) hundreds

of millions of e-mails virtually instantly. As more and more advertisers turn to

?
spam to sell their products, the e-mail that we want to receive (it) could be greatly

prep.
outnumbered (for) junk e-mail. Would you continue to use e-mail if you had to delete

prep. needed
100 pieces spam for each e-mail that was written to you by someone you know?

Mention computer viruses in   prep.
this para. Companies rely (with) e-mail for their employees to communicate with each

Add transition.
other. Spamming corrupts their internal communications, and they are unable to

prep. word form
communicate effectively. Such a situation results (with) a (lost) of productivity for the

word order
company and (requires sometimes) the company to reformulate its communication

network, (to.)

"Despite" never goes with "of"   *wrong word*

Despite of these problems for businesses, some people might (discuss) that
commercial speech the same as everyday speech?
criminalizing spam would infringe on spammers' right to free speech. However,

how free is speech that drowns out (another) voices that we want to hear? The right to

free speech does not allow companies to flood my mail box with (its) e-mail garbage.
?
prep.
Yes, free speech is an essential component of the exchange (with) ideas necessary
a
for flourishing democracy. Unsolicited e-mails, however, threaten to inhibit effective

communication, not nurture it.
of   *add an appropriate adjective*
Because these reasons, our lawmakers need to legislate against spam. Spammers

should be fined, and perhaps jailed, if they continue to disturb people with their
prep.
incessant pleas (of) our attention and our money. E-mail was designed (for) be a

helpful tool (for) allow people all over the world (too) communicate with each other
word forms   *Why THE?*
quick and effective, but spam threatens to destroy this advance in the human

communication.

What a GREAT discussion of this topic! I wholeheartedly agree with you.
Prepositions: Wow! You have at least 10 errors of this kind. As you revise,
study the corrections. Prepositions are difficult, but the errors really detract
from the quality of your essay.
Do you know the difference between because and because of? What about
the difference between despite and in spite of?
I look forward to reading your next draft!

Read the revised version of "Can Spam!" What has been changed? What still needs improvement?

Can Spam!

When I first got an e-mail account ten years ago, I received communications only from friends, family, and professional acquaintances. Businesses did not contact me with advertisements to sell me their services. Now it seems that every time I check my e-mail, I have to delete an endless **parade** of advertisements and other correspondence that does not come from legitimate businesses and therefore does not interest me at all. If we want e-mail to continue to be useful, we need specific laws that criminalize spam. The annoying avalanche of spam threatens to destroy this important means of modern communication.

If the government does not do something soon to outlaw spam, the problem will certainly get much worse. Computer programs allow spammers to send hundreds of millions of e-mails virtually instantly. As more and more advertisers turn to spam to sell their products, the e-mail that we want to receive could be greatly outnumbered by junk e-mail. Would you continue to use e-mail if you had to delete 100 pieces of spam for each e-mail that was written to you by someone you know?

Although this problem with e-mail is **troubling** for private individuals, it is even worse for large businesses. Many spam e-mails contain computer viruses that can shut down the entire network of a business. Companies rely on e-mail for their employees to communicate with each other. Spamming corrupts their internal communications, and a company's employees are thus unable to communicate effectively. Such a situation results in a loss of productivity for the company and sometimes requires the company to reformulate its communication network, too. These computer problems raise the company's costs, which must then be passed on to the consumer.

Despite these problems for businesses, some people might argue that criminalizing spam would infringe on spammers' right to free speech. However, how free is speech that drowns out other voices that we want to hear? Commercial speech that is designed to encourage people to spend money is legally different from people's right to voice their personal opinions. The right to free speech does not allow companies to flood my mailbox with their e-mail garbage. Yes, free speech is an essential component of the exchange of ideas necessary for a flourishing democracy. Unsolicited e-mails, however, threaten to inhibit effective communication, not to nurture it.

Because of these important reasons, our lawmakers need to legislate against spam. Spammers should be fined, and perhaps jailed, if they continue to disturb people with their incessant pleas for our attention and our money. E-mail was designed to be a helpful tool to allow people all over the world to communicate with one another quickly and effectively, but spam threatens to destroy this advance in human communication.

---

a parade: a long procession of things   **troubling:** causing distress or worry

Analyzing Content and Organization

ACTIVITY 7 Analyzing the Content

Answer these questions about the revised version (Essay 5C) of "Can Spam!"

1. How many paragraphs does this essay have? _____

2. What is the topic? _____

3. Write the thesis statement here. _____

   _____

4. What reasons does the writer give for her viewpoint?

   _____

   _____

   _____

   _____

5. After reading this student's essay, do you agree with her viewpoint in the conclusion? Why or why not?

   _____

   _____

   _____

6. If you disagree with the thesis, what could the writer have done to make her point more convincing? If you agree with the thesis, think of some ways in which the writer could have been even more convincing.

   _____

   _____

   _____

7. Does the last sentence in the conclusion offer a suggestion, an opinion, or a prediction?

   _____

Read the outline of "Can Spam!" Then use information in the box to complete the outline.

> - should be criminalized
> - lose productivity
> - background information
> - the right to fill people's e-mail accounts with spam
> - is growing

I. Introduction

    A. Give _____ about e-mail.

    B. Demonstrate that e-mail advertisements ("spam") have become a problem.

    C. Thesis statement: The avalanche of spam threatens to destroy this important means of communication.

II. Body Paragraph 1

    A. Show that the problem with spam _____

    B. Show that the problem with spam threatens the usefulness of e-mail as a means of communication.

III. Body Paragraph 2

    A. Show that the problem is potentially even more troublesome for businesses than for individuals.

    B. Discuss the ways in which businesses will _____ if employees spend time deleting spam.

IV. Body Paragraph 3

    A. Address a likely counterargument that spam is a mode of free speech.

    B. Demonstrate that a company's right to advertise does not give it _____ _____

V. Conclusion

    A. Suggest that spam _____

    B. Offer a prediction about the effect of not criminalizing spam.

⚒ Building Better Sentences

    Correct and varied sentence structure is essential to the quality of your writing. For further practice with "Can Spam!" go to Practice 5 on page 206 in Appendix 1.

Transitions and Connectors in Argumentative Essays

Transitional phrases and connectors in argumentative essays help the reader to follow the logical development of the argument. When you move from one paragraph to the next to further develop a point, use a word or phrase from the following list of transitions that develop a point further. When you move from one paragraph to the next to address or refute a counterargument, use a word or phrase from the list of transitions that address a counterargument.

Transitions and Connectors That Develop a Point Further	Transitions and Connectors That Address a Counterargument
additionally	although
also	but
besides	conversely
correspondingly	despite
furthermore	however
in a similar manner	in spite of
likewise	nevertheless
moreover	nonetheless
similarly	on the other hand
what is more	still
	though
	yet

ACTIVITY 9 Using Transitions and Connectors

Reread the revised version (Essay 5C) of "Can Spam!" on pages 118–119. Find and list four transitions or connectors and write the paragraph number after each one.

1. _____ ( )   3. _____ ( )

2. _____ ( )   4. _____ ( )

 For more practice with the structure of argumentative essays, try Unit 5, Activity 1 on the *Great Writing 5* Web site: elt.heinle.com/greatwriting

Building Better Grammar

This section will help you to refine your grammar skills and become a better editor of your own writing. (NOTE: See the Brief Writer's Handbook with Activities, pages 194–198, for additional grammar activities.)

Grammar Topic 5.1

Preposition Combinations

Prepositions are one of the most difficult parts of speech to learn in almost any language. Many times, it is necessary to memorize preposition combinations of *verb + preposition*, *noun + preposition*, and *adjective + preposition*. You need to practice these important combinations.

verb + preposition:	wait **for**, excel **in**, count **on**
noun + preposition:	the majority **of**, a need **for**, a solution **to**
adjective + preposition:	good **at**, excited **about**, proud **of**

ACTIVITY 10 Working with Preposition Combinations

Complete each sentence with the correct preposition. (NOTE: Many of these word combinations can be found in "Can Spam!" [version Essay 5C], pages 118–119.)

1. No businesses contacted me _____ advertisements to sell me their services.

2. an endless parade _____ advertisements

3. I have no interest _____ reading

4. hundreds _____ millions _____ e-mails

5. X is outnumbered _____ Y

6. 100 pieces _____ spam

7. e-mail that was written to you _____ someone you know

8. this problem is troubling _____ individuals

9. the potential _____ improvement

10. Companies rely _____ e-mail _____ their employees to communicate _____ each other.

11. a loss _____ productivity _____ the company

12. infringe _____ an advertiser's right _____ free speech

13. the exchange _____ ideas

14. it is necessary for the flourishing _____ a democracy

15. _____ these reasons

16. they continue to disturb us _____ their incessant pleas _____ our attention

Grammar Topic 5.2

Verb Tense with *If* in Future Time

In sentences with an *if*-clause, the *if*-clause is the condition. The other clause—the main clause—is the result.

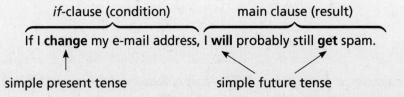

if-clause (condition)   main clause (result)

If I delete all my spam messages, I will have very few messages left.

Sentences with *if*-clauses can talk about the past, the present, or the future. When they talk about the future, the main clause expresses the simple future tense with *will* or with *be going* to. However, the *if*-clause uses the simple present tense to express what is clearly a future time.

if-clause (condition)   main clause (result)

If I **change** my e-mail address, I **will** probably still **get** spam.

simple present tense   simple future tense

Rule: In a sentence with an *if*-clause that expresses future time, use the simple future tense only in the main clause. Use the simple present tense in the *if*-clause. Do not use *will* in the *if*-clause.

A common use of *if* is in the present time. In this case, *if* is similar to *when* or *whenever* in meaning, and the verb in each clause is in the present tense.

If I **receive** an e-mail from an unknown sender, I immediately **delete** it.

simple present tense
(for a usual, repeated action)

For actions in the past, both clauses can use the simple past tense.

If you **used** instant messaging, the other person **got** the message immediately.

simple past tense

(NOTE: None of these uses of *if* involves contrary-to-fact situations.)

ACTIVITY 11 Working with Verb Tense with *If*

Each of the following sentences contains a verb tense error. Circle the error and write the correction above it.

1. If something will not be done soon, the problem could get much worse.

2. If spamming will corrupt their internal communications, they will be unable to communicate effectively.

3. Spammers should be fined, and perhaps jailed, if they will continue to disturb people with their incessant pleas for our attention and our money.

4. If we will not do something about spam now, the problem will get much worse before it gets better.

5. If people wanted to communicate with each other before 1980, they will use the telephone or the post office.

 For more practice with *if*-clauses, try Unit 5, Activity 2 on the *Great Writing 5* Web site: elt.heinle.com/greatwriting

ACTIVITY 12 Working with Real Language Use

Look in newspapers, in magazines, and on the Internet to locate three examples of sentences with if-clauses in future time. Write the examples below. Circle the verb in each clause and write its tense. Finally, identify the source of your sentences. Give the name of the source, its date, and the page number.

1. Sentence: _____

_____

Verb tense of main clause: _____

Verb tense of *if*-clause: _____

Source information: _____

_____

2. Sentence: _____

_____

Verb tense of main clause: _____

Verb tense of *if*-clause: _____

Source information: _____

_____

3. Sentence: _____

_____

Verb tense of main clause: _____

Verb tense of *if*-clause: _____

Source information: _____

_____

Grammar Topic 5.3
Because and *Because Of*

The Conjunction Because

Because is a conjunction. It connects a dependent clause to a main clause. (Any sentence that has a *because*-clause must have another clause.) The clause that begins with *because* can be at the beginning or at the end of a sentence.

Rule 1: *Because* is followed by a subject + verb.

because   +   subject   +   verb

We need laws that criminalize spam **because** the <u>avalanche</u> of spam <u>threatens</u> to destroy this important means of communication.

Rule 2: A sentence with a *because*-clause must have another clause.

Because the <u>avalanche</u> of spam <u>threatens</u> to destroy this important means of communication, <u>we</u> <u>need</u> laws that criminalize spam.

second clause

The Preposition Because Of

Because of is a preposition. It must have a noun (or a pronoun) after it. The prepositional phrase with *because of* can be at the beginning or end of the sentence.

Rule 3: *Because of* is always followed by a noun or a pronoun.

because of   +   noun

My favorite writer is William Shakespeare **because of** <u>the beautiful language</u> and <u>the strong characters</u> in his works.

noun

NOTE: The location of a clause with *because* or a phrase with *because of* can vary depending on how the sentence best fits in the paragraph or essay. When a clause with *because* or a phrase with *because of* comes at the beginning of a sentence, it is followed by a comma.

Because of the beautiful language and the strong characters in his works, my favorite writer is William Shakespeare. (comma)

OR

My favorite writer is William Shakespeare **because of** the beautiful language and the strong characters in his works. (no comma)

Complete each sentence with because *or* because of.

1. I had to call my Internet provider _____ my e-mail account was filled with spam.

2. At times, users may receive a message that says, "Your Internet connection was interrupted _____ a program error or user inactivity."

3. _____ Internet glitches, the software company had no choice but to withdraw a security improvement.

4. As the year 2000 approached, international defense agencies beefed up computer security tremendously _____ widespread belief that attacks on them would increase.

5. Spam is a tremendous financial nuisance to carriers and recipients of the messages _____ most of the costs are incurred by the carriers and recipients instead of the senders.

6. One of the largest Internet providers in Asia recently began to block e-mail from a certain company called Krickland Enterprises _____ the provider had received numerous complaints from its subscribers about spam being sent to them from this company's addresses.

7. A recent study has found that 30% of survey respondents indicated that they use e-mail less _____ the alarming wave of spam that is flooding into Internet users' boxes.

8. _____ no spam filter is perfect, it is likely that spam will continue to be a problem for all Internet users.

For more practice with *because* and *because of*, try Unit 5, Activity 3 on the *Great Writing 5* Web site: elt.heinle.com/greatwriting

Grammar Topic 5.4
Confusing Words: *To/Too/Two*

The words *to, too,* and *two* sound alike, but they are used very differently. Do not confuse them in your writing.

to = preposition	The plan will give more money **to** schools.
infinitive	If voters want better schools, they have **to pay** more taxes.
too = adverb (means *also*)	Our plan is weak, but their plan is weak, **too**.
adverb (means *very*)	If taxes are **too** high, voters may be angry.
two = a number	There were **two** possible ways to solve the problem.

ACTIVITY 14 Working with Confusing Words: *To/Too/Two*

Complete each sentence with to, too, *or* two.

1. What can we do _____ solve the problem of spam?

2. Please submit _____ copies of your application. One should go _____ the registrar, and the other should go _____ your advisor.

3. If _____ people apply for the same job, a committee of five meets _____ decide _____ whom they should give the position.

4. If you would like _____ support this plan because you believe that it is _____ risky _____ continue with our current situation, then please sign this petition. If you have friends or acquaintances who might be interested in this, please ask them to sign, _____.

Grammar Topic 5.5
Word Parts

You can increase your vocabulary in two basic ways. One way is to learn words that you have never seen before. The second way is to learn word parts, which will help you to understand how other words are constructed. Recognizing word parts and using them correctly will increase your vocabulary and thus improve your writing.

NOTE: See the Brief Writer's Handbook with Activities, pages 192–193, for more information on word parts.

Read the following paragraph. Five of the eight underlined words contain an error with word parts. Correct the error or write C (correct).

Interviews in Data Collection

Personal interviews are generally considered to be one of the most (1.) <u>validity</u>

_____ methods of survey research. In a (2.) <u>personal</u>

_____ interview, the (3.) <u>interview</u> _____

can probe, ask for (4.) <u>clarification</u> _____, clear up any misunderstandings

(5.) <u>immediate</u> _____, ensure that all questions are answered

completely, and pursue (6.) <u>unexpect</u> _____ avenues. Thus, data

(7.) <u>result</u> _____ from an interview are often of a higher (8.) <u>quality</u>

_____ than data resulting from a questionnaire.

Seven of the following ten sentences contain an error involving one of the grammar topics featured in this unit. Write C before the three correct sentences. Write X before the incorrect sentences, circle the error, and write a correction above it.

_____ 1. The number of spam e-mails is certainly a problem, but the inappropriate content of many of these messages is a problem, to.

_____ 2. If your computer seems to have a problem with a virus, you should get in contact with your local computer repair shop as soon as possible.

_____ 3. The spectators at the gymnastics competition expressed their disapproval because the extremely low score that the judges awarded.

_____ 4. If there will be sufficient demand for a new type of spam blocker, one of the major computer companies will market it.

_____ 5. It is a teacher's job to teach well, but ultimately students are responsible to how much they are able to learn in a course.

_____ 6. Because the manufacturer's decision to cut product prices in half, consumers now have the opportunity to purchase a great new car at a very reasonable price.

_____ 7. Because of a major increase in the number of people using the Internet, e-mail has become the main means of communication for many people.

_____ 8. Disappointed with his team's performance in the match, the coach blamed the loss on the poor performance of three key players.

_____ 9. Because of people were becoming annoyed with the amount of spam in their e-mail accounts, they asked their government officials to pass some kind of law to solve their dilemma.

_____ 10. The dentist told her patient, "Take one of these tablets for the next week. Come back for a follow-up visit next Wednesday. If you will have any problems between now and then, call us immediately."

For more practice with the grammar topics from this unit, try Unit 5, Activity 4 on the *Great Writing 5* Web site: elt.heinle.com/greatwriting

Seven of the ten underlined words in the following paragraph contain an error involving one of the grammar topics featured in this unit. Correct the errors on the lines provided. If the word or phrase is correct, write C.

EXAMPLE PARAGRAPH

International Advertising

Advertising programs in foreign markets need (1.) <u>to</u> _____ take a number of

key (2.) <u>considers</u> _____ into account. First, a broad vision of sales in international

markets is a requirement. This means, among other things, that overseas markets must be viewed with

promise if the marketing challenges are to be properly faced. Second, international advertising rarely

succeeds if it (3.) <u>will be</u> _____ merely a duplicate (4.) <u>of</u> _____

advertising used in the United States. (5.) <u>Traditional</u> _____, religions, and

economic conditions may dictate the (6.) <u>natural</u> _____ of the sales appeal.

Illustrations should fit local conditions with respect (7.) <u>about</u> _____ such

matters as color preferences and taboos. Advertising in India, for example, should never show the

cow (8.) <u>because of</u> _____ it is a sacred animal. Finally, difficulties in translation

must be considered, (9.) <u>too</u> _____. Communication can be (10.) <u>serious</u>

_____ impaired and even prevented if a single word is mistranslated.

ACTIVITY 18 Word Associations

Circle the word or phrase that is most closely related to the word or phrase on the left. If necessary, use a dictionary to check the meaning of words you do not know.

#	Word	Option 1	Option 2
1.	acquaintances	people	things
2.	to delete	to add	to subtract
3.	a parade	one person	many people
4.	correspondence	spoken words	written words
5.	to criminalize	to make illegal	to make legal
6.	virtually	almost	completely
7.	to outnumber	as many as	more than
8.	troubling	it bothers you	you bother it
9.	such	for example	for good
10.	to reformulate	to do the form again	to make a plan again
11.	to infringe	to expand	to limit
12.	to drown out	to cover	to reveal
13.	essential	optional	required
14.	flourishing	prospering	surprising
15.	unsolicited	not requested	not understood
16.	to inhibit	to provide	to constrain
17.	to nurture	to help to grow	to persuade to act
18.	to fine	to charge a penalty	to locate easily
19.	incessant	irregular	unending
20.	a plea	a strong request	a strong punishment

Fill in each blank with the word or phrase on the left that most naturally completes the phrase on the right. If necessary, use a dictionary to check the meaning of words you do not know.

1. professional / natural   _____ acquaintances

2. an old e-mail / a friend   to delete _____

3. satisfactory / perfect   virtually _____

4. family / plan   to reformulate my _____

5. noise / success   to drown out _____

6. candy / talk   incessant _____

7. delicious / important   _____ correspondence

8. on / to   to infringe _____

9. ingredient / mistake   an essential _____

10. for / of   a plea _____ assistance

11. avenue / majority   the _____ of the population

12. decide / solve   to _____ a dilemma

13. complaining / gratitude   incessant _____

14. essential / event   an alarming _____

15. convince / excel   to _____ in something

16. cheap / free   _____ speech

17. communication / explanation   a means of _____

18. greatly / poorly   _____ outnumbered

19. because / despite   _____ of

20. for / of   X is a duplicate _____ Y

Original Student Writing: Argumentative Essay

In this section, you will follow the seven steps in the writing process to write an argumentative essay. To review the details of each step, see Unit 1, pages 7–13.

ACTIVITY 20 Original Argumentative Essay

Using the seven steps that follow, write an argumentative essay.

Step 1: Choose a Topic

Your first step is to choose a topic for your essay. Choose a topic that you understand well, including both sides of the issue. Your teacher may assign a topic, you may think of one yourself, or you may choose one from the suggestions below. As you consider possible topics, ask yourself, "What do I know about this topic? What do my readers know? What else do I need to know? Even though I know this topic well, is there additional information that I need in order to explain the topic better to my readers?"

Humanities	Present an argument about the quality of a recent movie. Should your readers see the movie or not?
Sciences	Is it ethical to clone animals? Write an argumentative essay that addresses this topic.
Business	Describe the best strategies that managers should use to motivate their employees.
Personal	Who is your personal hero? Explain why this person inspires you.

1. What topic did you choose? _____

2. Why did you choose this topic? _____

   _____

   _____

   _____

3. How well do you know this topic? What is your experience with it?

   _____

   _____

Step 2: Brainstorm

Use this space to jot down as many ideas about the topic as you can.

Brainstorming Box

Step 3: Outline

Prepare a simple outline of your essay. (This outline is for five paragraphs, but you may have more or fewer if your teacher approves.)

Title: _____

I. Introduction

    A. Hook: _____

    _____

    B. Connecting information: _____

    _____

    _____

    C. Thesis statement: _____

    _____

II. Body Paragraph 1 (Point 1): _____

    A. _____

    _____

    B. _____

    _____

III. Body Paragraph 2 (Point 2): _____

    A. _____

    _____

    B. _____

    _____

IV. Body Paragraph 3 (Point 3): _____

    A. _____

    _____

    B. _____

    _____

V. Conclusion: _____

    _____

Peer Editing of Outlines

Exchange books with a partner. Read your partner's outline. Then use the following questions to help you to comment on your partner's outline. Use your partner's feedback to revise your outline.

1. Is there any aspect of the outline that looks unclear to you?

_____

_____

_____

_____

2. Can you think of an area in the outline that needs more development? Do you have any specific suggestions?

_____

_____

_____

_____

3. If you have any other ideas or suggestions, write them here.

_____

_____

_____

_____

Step 4: Write the First Draft

Use the information from Steps 1, 2, and 3 to write the first draft of your argumentative essay. Use at least five of the vocabulary words or phrases presented in Activity 18 and Activity 19. Underline these words and phrases in your essay.

Step 5: Get Feedback from a Peer

Exchange papers from Step 4 with a partner. Read your partner's writing. Then use Peer Editing Sheet 5 on page 217 to help you to comment on your partner's writing. Be sure to offer positive suggestions and comments that will help your partner improve his or her writing.

Step 6: Revise the First Draft

Read the comments on Peer Editing Sheet 5 about your essay. Then reread your essay. Can you identify places where you plan to make revisions? List the improvements you are going to make.

1. _____

_____

_____

2. _____

_____

_____

3. _____

_____

_____

Use all the information from the previous steps to write the final version of your paper. Often, writers will need to write a third or even fourth draft to express their ideas as clearly as possible. Write as many drafts as necessary to produce a good essay.

Step 7: Proofread the Final Draft

Be sure to proofread your paper several times before you submit it.

Additional Topics for Writing

Here are ten topics for additional argumentative essay writing.

TOPIC 1: Why senior citizens should or should not be allowed to retain their drivers' licenses

TOPIC 2: Why computers in public libraries should or should not have Internet filters installed

TOPIC 3: Why your class should take a field trip to a particular place

TOPIC 4: Why television shows should or should not be allowed to use obscene language

TOPIC 5: Why your college major should change its course requirements

TOPIC 6: Why the military draft should or should not be reinstated

TOPIC 7: Why public schools should or should not offer bilingual programs

TOPIC 8: Why junk food manufacturers should or should not be allowed to advertise their products to children

TOPIC 9: Why a friend of yours should or should not enroll in your college

TOPIC 10: Why health care should or should not be provided by the government

Timed Writing

How quickly can you write in English? There are many times when you must write quickly, such as on a test. It is important to feel comfortable during those times. Timed-writing practice can make you feel better about writing quickly in English.

First, read the essay guidelines below. Then take out a piece of paper. Read the writing prompt below the guidelines. As quickly as you can, write a basic outline for this writing prompt (including the thesis and your three main points). You should spend <u>no more than</u> 5 minutes on your outline.

You will then have 40 minutes to write a 5-paragraph argumentative essay about your topic. At the end of the 40 minutes, your teacher will collect your work and return it to you at a later date.

Argumentative Essay Guidelines

- Be sure to present and refute a counterargument in your body.

- Remember to give your essay a title.

- Double-space your essay.

- Write as legibly as possible (if you are not using a computer).

- Include a short introduction (with a thesis statement), three body paragraphs, and a conclusion.

- Try to give yourself a few minutes before the end of the activity to review your work. Check for spelling, verb tense, and subject-verb agreement mistakes.

> Should people eat a vegetarian diet? Write an argumentative
> essay for or against vegetarianism.

Narrative Essays

GOAL: To learn how to write a narrative essay

*Grammar Topics: **6.1** Unclear pronoun usage; **6.2** Expressing past time: simple past, past progressive, past perfect tenses; **6.3** *-ly* adverbs for advanced writing; **6.4** Confusing words: *we're/were/where*; **6.5** Word parts

What Is a Narrative Essay?

A **narrative essay** is a nonfictional account of an experience. Narrative essays could describe a trip that you took or a particular memory from your childhood. A narrative essay might tell a story about your family or explain how a certain event influenced your development into the person you now are. You have as many narrative essays to write as you have lifetime experiences. Through narrative essays, writers share events that happened to them to explain the ways in which they perceive the world.

How Is a Narrative Essay Organized?

As with any essay, a narrative essay has a thesis statement so that its relevance and meaning are apparent to the reader. You could write a narrative essay about going to the store to buy butter, but unless something truly unexpected or remarkable happened during the errand, this life experience is not the most interesting one to describe. Narrative essays are more interesting and enjoyable when the writers share the reason that the experience is important to their growth and maturity. This reason should be the thesis of your narrative essay.

Narrative essays contain an introduction, supporting body paragraphs, and a conclusion. The body of a narrative essay tells the plot of your story and gives supporting details and evidence to bolster the thesis of the essay. Since narrative essays tell a story, you also need to consider these additional elements:

Setting	The setting is the location of the narrative. Where does the story take place?
Main Characters	The main characters are the people described in the narrative essay. Who are the essential actors in the story?
Plot	The plot is the action and events of the narrative essay. What happened to the main characters?
Climax	The climax is the most interesting or exciting point of the plot. What is the narrative essay's single most dramatic, tense, or engaging moment?
Ending	The ending is the resolution of the story, also called the denouement. How are the issues in the plot resolved?

Topics for Narrative Essays

What is a good topic for a narrative essay? What are the stories about your life that you find yourself telling again and again? The answers to these two questions are the same. A narrative is a story, so the topic of a narrative essay should tell about an interesting or significant event in your life.

Here are some general topics that lend themselves well to a narrative essay:

- a memorable family holiday

- a special vacation or trip

- the first time you did something, such as skiing or wallpapering a room

- an unexpected event

- a time that you learned an important lesson

ACTIVITY 1 Identifying Appropriate Topics for Narrative Essay

Read these eight topics. Put a check mark (✔) next to the four that could be good topics for narrative essays.

_____ 1. the steps in making my favorite dish

_____ 2. my brother's wedding day

_____ 3. my experience as a babysitter

_____ 4. illustrations in children's storybooks

_____ 5. an argument against cloning

_____ 6. a soldier's first week in battle

_____ 7. the history of a foreign country

_____ 8. disasters during a family vacation

Think of two additional topics that would be appropriate for a narrative essay.

9. _____

10. _____

Supporting Details

After you have selected the topic of your narrative essay, your task is to identify the **setting, main characters, plot, climax,** and **ending.** This process will also help you to identify supporting details for your essay. What are the details of the event that make it interesting and unique? What would readers like to learn about the topic?

Do you have a favorite story from your childhood? Can you think of an important and memorable event in your life? Use one or both of the boxes below to write some ideas about a story from your life. Be sure to include the reason that you like this story. Can this reason become the thesis statement of your essay?

an important and memorable event in your life	
a list of episodes in the narrative	
why you like this story and why it is important to you	

You can brainstorm the same information in terms of the parts of a story.

Setting	
Main Characters	
Plot	
Climax	
Ending	

Studying a Sample Narrative Essay

In this section, you will study three versions of a narrative essay: a first draft, the same first draft with teacher comments, and the revised essay.

ACTIVITY 3 Warming Up to the Topic

Answer these questions individually. Then discuss them with a partner or in a small group.

1. Why do people learn a second language? _____

   _____

2. What are some reasons that people do not succeed at learning a second language?

   _____

   _____

   _____

3. How do you think learning a second language is different now from the way it was one hundred years

   ago? _____

   _____

   _____

   _____

   _____

As you read this first draft, look for areas that need improvement.

Why I Learned English

My family's roots are mixed and **intertwined** with several different **ethnic** and culture background. My mother's parents are American, but her ancestors are origin from England and German. My father's mother is Peruvian, but his father is Egyptian. I grew up in Peru with my parents in a quiet neighborhood of Lima. My **paternal** grandparents lived down the street from us, but my **maternal** grandparents lived in America. I didn't learn English for school; I learned English so that I spoke to my grandparents.

When my maternal grandparents would fly from North America to South America to visit us, my mother had to translate among the different family members. We spoke Spanish in our house, but my American grandparents spoke only English. Since he did not speak a word of Spanish. My mother was constantly **interpreting** questions and answers. I hated this translation step so much that I was determined that one day I will be able to speak to my grandparents by myself.

Eventually, this situation reached its **boiling point.** One day my mother asked to my grandmother to pick me up from school. My school was only a few blocks from our house. But my grandmother got horrible lost in the way. She ended up in the wrong neighborhood. She had to get help from the police. Now we all realized that being **monolingual** was a huge **handicap.** In addition, it was a potential dangerous handicap!

The next time my grandparents came to visit, I taped vocabulary cards on all of the objects in our house. On the *silla*, I hung a card with "chair" written on it. On the *mesa*, I attached a card that said "table." I continued putting these English words in the house. Meanwhile, my grandparents saw how hardly I was working for learn English, and they had decided that they wanted to learn Spanish. Later, we wrote the Spanish words on all of the cards as well so that we could practice together. Most of the cards we're yellow, and I used a green pen to write the words. My mom would help us with grammar whenever we had questions. It was so much fun to turn our monolingual Spanish house into a truly bilingual home.

During I was studying English, I realized that learn a language does more than teach you the new words; it ables you to learn about the new people. Instead of need my mother to say me stories about my grandparents, we can now talk direct each other. By learn new things, you can to experience new relationships.

---

intertwined: joined by twisting together

ethnic: relating to a group of people who share the same racial, national, religious, linguistic, or cultural background

paternal: related through one's father

maternal: related through one's mother

interpret: to explain the meaning

a boiling point: a critical moment, a climax

monolingual: using only one language

a handicap: something that gets in the way, a disadvantage

Read the teacher comments on the first draft of "Why I Learned English." Are these the same things that you noticed?

Why I Learned English

What about a more generic intro so you can move from PEOPLE to YOUR FAMILY to YOU?

redundant

My family's roots are (mixed and intertwined) with several different ethnic

word forms and cultur(e)background. My mother's parents are American, but her ancestors

adverb are origin from England and German. My father's mother is Peruvian, but his father

is Egyptian. I grew up in Peru with my parents in a quiet neighborhood of Lima.

My paternal grandparents lived down the street from us, but my maternal

grandparents lived in America. I didn't learn English for school; I learned English so

add modal "could" that I (spoke) to my grandparents.

This para. needs a topic sentence. When my maternal grandparents would fly from North America to South

America to visit us, my mother had to translate among the different family members.

We spoke Spanish in our house, but my American grandparents spoke only English.

FRAG Since (he)did not speak a word of Spanish. My mother was constantly interpreting

questions and answers. I hated this translation step so much that I was determined

tense? that one day I (will)be able to speak to my grandparents by myself.

Eventually, this situation reached its boiling point. One day my mother asked(to)

my grandmother to pick me up from school. My school was only a few blocks from

combine *word form* *prep* our house. But my grandmother got horr(i)ble lost (in)the way. She ended up in the

combine—choppy wrong neighborhood. She had to get help from the police. Now we all realized that

being monolingual was a huge han<u>dic</u>ap. In <u>addition</u>, it was a poten(tial)dangerous

Put this info in previous sentence.

han<u>dic</u>ap!

Connect this idea more directly to your thesis about learning languages in your previous paragraph.

∧ The next time my grandparents came to visit, I taped vocabulary cards on

Transition sentence? This is a huge leap.

all of the objects in our house. On the *silla*, I hung a card with "chair" written on it.

On the *mesa*, I attached a card that said "table." I continued putting these English

all over?

words <u>in</u> the house. Meanwhile, my grandparents saw how hard(ly) I was working

why past perfect?

(for) learn English, and they <u>had decided</u> that they wanted to learn Spanish. Later, we

wrote the Spanish words on all of the cards as well so that we could practice together.

Is this important? relevant? Can you develop / use it better in the essay?

<u>Most of the cards (we're) yellow, and I used a green pen to write the words.</u> My mom

would help us with grammar whenever we had questions. It was so much fun to turn

our monolingual Spanish house into a truly bilingual home.

word choice?   *word form*

<u>During</u> I was studying English, I realized that le(arn) a language does more than

not a verb   *word form*

teach you the new words; it <u>ables</u> you to learn about t/he new people. Instead of ne(ed)

word choice

my mother to <u>say</u> me stories about my grandparents, we can now talk direct(t) each

other. By lear(n) new things, you can to experience new relationships.

This is an interesting story. It's easy for your reader to follow.

My main suggestion to improve your writing is to combine some of your sentences.

You have 2 fragments—VERY SERIOUS ERRORS. If you need help with fragments, see grammar point 4.2 in this textbook.

Read the revised version of "Why I Learned English." What has been changed? What still needs improvement?

Why I Learned English

Many families reflect diverse cultural backgrounds that come together. My family's roots are intertwined with several different ethnic and cultural backgrounds. My mother's parents are American, but her ancestors are originally from England and Germany. My father's mother is Peruvian, but his father is Egyptian. I grew up in Peru with my parents in a quiet neighborhood of Lima. My paternal grandparents lived down the street from us, but my maternal grandparents lived in the United States. Unlike most non-native speakers, I did not learn English just to get a good grade in school; I learned English so that I could speak to my grandparents.

Coming from a multilingual family sparked many difficulties in communication. For example, when my maternal grandparents would fly from North America to South America to visit us, my mother had to translate among the different family members. We spoke Spanish in our house, but my American grandparents spoke only English. Since they did not speak a word of Spanish, my mother was constantly interpreting questions and answers. Rather than enjoying their visit, my mother had to work as a translator. With my mom's help, I could understand my grandparents, but I wanted to be able to speak to them by myself.

Eventually, this situation reached its boiling point. One day my mother asked my grandmother to pick me up from school. My school was only a few blocks from our house, but my grandmother got horribly lost on the way. She ended up in the wrong neighborhood and had to get help from the police. It was quite embarrassing for a grown woman to find herself lost in a small neighborhood. Now we all realized that being monolingual was a huge handicap. In addition, it was a potentially dangerous **liability**!

Because of this incident, I decided to take action. The next time my grandparents came to visit, I taped vocabulary cards on all of the objects in our house. On the *silla*, I hung a card with "chair" written on it. On the *mesa*, I attached a card that said "table." I continued putting these English words all over the house. Meanwhile, my grandparents saw how hard I was working to learn English, and they decided that they wanted to learn Spanish. Later, we wrote the Spanish words on all of the cards as well so that we could practice together. My mom would help us with grammar whenever we had questions. It was so much fun to turn our monolingual Spanish house into a truly bilingual home.

While I was studying English, I realized that learning a language does more than teach you new words; it enables you to learn about new people. Instead of needing my mother to tell me stories about my grandparents, we can now talk directly to each other. Now my grandparents and I talk on the phone every week without a translator, and our relationship is much closer than it ever was before. By learning a common language to communicate, you can experience new relationships.

a liability: a disadvantage or handicap

Analyzing Content and Organization

Answer these questions about the revised version (Essay 6C) of "Why I Learned English."

1. Why did the narrator want to learn English? _____

   _____

   _____

2. How well does the first sentence of the essay grab your attention? Does it make you want to read the rest of the essay? _____

   _____

   _____

3. What is the setting of this narrative essay? Who are the main characters?

   _____

   _____

   _____

4. What is the plot of this narrative essay? What is its climax?

   _____

   _____

   _____

   _____

   _____

5. Does the essay have a thesis? What do you think the writer wants you to learn from reading this essay?

   _____

   _____

   _____

Read the outline of "Why I Learned English." Then use the information in the box to complete this outline for the essay.

> • Body Paragraph 3
>
> • the importance of learning a foreign language
>
> • characters
>
> • I could not communicate with my grandparents
>
> • my grandmother got lost

I. Introduction

   A. Provide background information about my family heritage.

   B. Introduce the setting and _____

   C. Thesis statement: My family heritage made learning English essential.

II. Body Paragraph 1: Establish the conflict of the plot: _____

   _____

III. Body Paragraph 2: Describe the climax: when _____

IV. _____: Tell the resolution and the solutions that we used to solve

   our problem.

V. Conclusion

   A. Summarize _____

   B. Explain how a person becomes open to new experiences with a new language.

Building Better Sentences

   Correct and varied sentence structure is essential to the quality of your writing. For further practice with "Why I Learned English," go to Practice 6 on page 207 in Appendix 1.

Transitions and Connectors in Narrative Essays

The most commonly used transitions and connectors in narrative essays are time words and phrases. Because a narrative essay tells a story, the transitions need to show sequence of events.

Time Words and Phrases		
after	following	one day
after that	from . . . to . . .	soon
at first	last	then
before	later	until
during	meanwhile	when
eventually	next, the next time	whenever
finally	now	while

ACTIVITY 9 Using Transitions and Connectors

Reread the revised version (Essay 6C) of "Why I Learned English" on pages 148–149. Find and list eight transitions or connectors and write the paragraph number after each one. The first one has been done for you.

1. _____when_____ (2)   5. _____ ( )

2. _____ ( )   6. _____ ( )

3. _____ ( )   7. _____ ( )

4. _____ ( )   8. _____ ( )

For more practice with structure of narrative essays, try Unit 6, Activity 1 on the *Great Writing 5* Web site: elt.heinle.com/greatwriting

Building Better Grammar

This section will help you to refine your grammar skills and become a better editor of your own writing. (NOTE: See the Brief Writer's Handbook with Activities, pages 194–198, for additional grammar activities.)

Grammar Topic 6.1

Unclear Pronoun Usage

When you use a pronoun, make sure that the reader knows which previously mentioned noun the pronoun refers to. If the pronoun's reference is ambiguous, use a noun.

Unclear: The banker told the customer that **he** could not accept coins, only paper money.
(Who is *he*? The banker? The customer?)

Clear: The banker told **the customer**, "I will not accept coins, only paper."

Unclear: **They** say that aspirin can help prevent heart attacks.
(Who is *they*?)

Clear: **Doctors** say that aspirin can help prevent heart attacks.

Unclear: The government passed the new law on July 17, **which** was surprising.
(What was surprising? The date? The law? The fact that the government passed the law?)

Clear: It was surprising that the government passed the new law on July 17 **rather than next fall.**
OR
The new law, which the government passed on July 17, was surprising.

Unclear: **They** may approve a contract for a new book when the authors submit a detailed summary of their proposed book.
(Who is *they*? The authors? The publishers?)

Clear: **Publishers** may approve a contract for a new book when the authors submit a detailed summary of their proposed book.

Unclear: "May I help you? We have hot dogs, hamburgers, and cheeseburgers."
"Yes, give me **one.**"
(What is *one*? A hot dog? A hamburger? A cheeseburger?)

Clear: "May I help you? We have hot dogs, hamburgers, and cheeseburgers."
"Yes, give me a **cheeseburger.**"

The correct possessive adjective when referring to *each, someone, somebody, anyone, anybody, everyone,* and *everybody* is *his* (or *her*). In conversational English, you will hear people use *their*, but this is not acceptable in formal academic writing.

Informal: Someone left **their** umbrella here.

Formal: Someone left **his** umbrella here.
OR
Someone left **his** or **her** umbrella here.

Best: Someone left **an** umbrella here.

NOTE: Using a possessive adjective with general nouns such as *someone* or *everybody* is awkward. *Their* is incorrect in formal writing. *His* omits half the population even though we do not know that the owner is male. *His or her* is wordy. The best solution is to avoid this construction when possible. One good way to avoid the necessity of referring to a singular word when you are talking about a group is to make the nouns plural. Instead of asking "Does each student have his or her book now?" it is easier to make the question plural and ask, "Do all students have their books now?"

Rewrite these sentences to create clear pronoun references.

1. When Michael drove his truck through the garage door, he damaged it.

   _____

2. When the Prince finds Cinderella, they can expect them to live happily ever after.

   _____

3. If your pet will not eat its food, then put it in the refrigerator.

   _____

4. In today's job market, a college graduate can find a good job more easily than a person who does not have one.

   _____

5. Both Susan Jennings and Kathy Miller teach at a college in central Turkey. She is a professor of chemistry.

   _____

6. They think that the criminal might have murdered as many as seven people.

   _____

7. Once everyone has their pencils sharpened, we may begin.

   _____

8. Mr. Johnston threw a party and made his special barbecued chicken, which we appreciated.

   _____

9. Last month the pilot flew to Rio and the following week to Paris. It is his favorite flight.

   _____

10. The professor verified whether or not everyone had done their homework.

    _____

For more practice with unclear pronoun reference, try Unit 6, Activity 2 on the *Great Writing 5* Web site: elt.heinle.com/greatwriting

Grammar Topic 6.2

Expressing Past Time: Simple Past, Past Progressive, Past Perfect Tenses

There are several ways of expressing past time in English.

Simple Past Tense

The most commonly used verb tense is the **simple past tense.** It often ends in *-ed* (*showed*) but can be irregular (*went*).

> In 1975, Harvey's Sandwich Shop **opened** its first store in this area of the country.

> In the twentieth century, automobiles **began** to transform transportation throughout the world.

Past Progressive Tense

This tense consists of *was* or *were* plus the verb + *-ing* form (*was eating, were playing*). The past progressive is used when a second action (expressed in the simple past) interrupts the flow of the action.

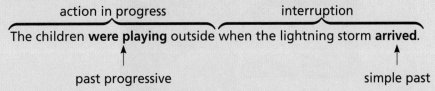

The children **were playing** outside when the lightning storm **arrived**.

past progressive   simple past

Past Perfect Tense

This tense consists of *had* plus the past participle form of the verb (*had eaten, had opened*). The past perfect tense is generally used in two cases.

1. When one past action occurred before another past action

> Zachary **received** a B+ on his test today because he **had studied** for three days in a row.

simple past   past perfect
(2nd action)   (1st action)

When it is clear to the reader which of the two past actions happened first, the past perfect is often optional. In the example below, the time word *before* makes the sequence of events clear.

> Zachary **received** a B+ on his test today because he **studied** for three days in a row the week <u>before</u>.

2. In *if*-clauses to describe a past unreal condition

> If Zachary **had studied** during the whole semester, he probably would have received an A.

NOTE: The past perfect is always mandatory here.

Read this paragraph about a famous pizza company that is known for its astute marketing strategies.
Underline the correct verb in each set of parentheses.

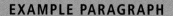

EXAMPLE PARAGRAPH

The Successful Development of New Products

Before launching any new product, Raphael's Pizza Company always (1. gathers / gathered /

had gathered) data by asking selected groups of people about the concept and the taste. For

example, before introducing their new Milan basil-flavored crust pizza, the company (2. elicits /

elicited / was eliciting) comments from groups of consumers, analyzed the results, and then

(3. invites / invited / was inviting / had invited) other groups to taste and discuss various samples.

Finally, Raphael's Pizza Company (4. tests / tested / was testing / had tested) actual customer

response by offering the product in a limited number of stores before the company (5. makes /

made / was making / had made) it available throughout the North America.

For more practice with expressing past time, try Unit 6, Activity 3 on the *Great Writing 5* Web site:
elt.heinle.com/greatwriting

Grammar Topic 6.3

-ly Adverbs for Advanced Writing

One of the best ways to make your writing more precise and at the same time to sound more formal and advanced is to use adverbs of manner and degree. The form of these adverbs is easy to learn because they end in *-ly*.

Adverbs of Manner

Adverbs of manner tell *how*.

adverb   adverb   verb
↓   ↓   ↓

The thief **quickly** and **quietly** <u>entered</u> the building.

verb adverb
↓   ↓

The project <u>ended</u> **badly**.

Adverbs of Degree

Adverbs of degree tell *to what extent*. They occur most often before adjectives, especially past participles used as adjectives. Instead of using the common word *very* in your essays, make your writing more original and more advanced by using other adverbs of degree.

adverb   adjective (past participle)
↓   ↓

The audience was **thoroughly** <u>disgusted</u> by the speaker's remarks.

adverb   adjective (past participle)
↓   ↓

Tracy Jenks is an **internationally** <u>recognized</u> expert in antiterrorism.

Common Adverbs of Degree			
adequately	extremely	partially	thoroughly
completely	greatly	particularly	tremendously
entirely	immensely	practically	virtually
especially	internationally	profoundly	widely

Underline the correct word in each set of parentheses.

EXAMPLE PARAGRAPH

Delivering Bad News to Employees

In a company, how should bad news be reported to employees? The (1. bad / badly) news is communicated up front in (2. direct / directly) written messages. Even in an (3. indirect / indirectly) written message, if you have done a (4. convincing / convincingly) job of explaining the reasons, the bad news itself will (5. natural / naturally) come as no surprise; the decision will appear (6. logical / logically) and reasonable—indeed the only logical and (7. reasonable / reasonably) decision that could have been made under the circumstances. Readers should not be (8. tremendous / tremendously) shocked by any sudden news. To retain the reader's goodwill, state the bad news in (9. positive / positively) or (10. neutral / neutrally) language, stressing what you are able to do rather than what you are not able to do. In addition, put the bad news in the middle of a paragraph and include additional discussion of reasons in the same sentence or (11. immediate / immediately) afterward. People may (12. great / greatly) appreciate news that is delivered in this direct way—no matter how bad it is.

Writer's Note

Remembering to Include *-ly* Adverbs

When you want your writing to sound more advanced, use *-ly* adverbs. Remember that *-ly* adverbs include both adverbs of manner (*slowly, carefully*) and adverbs of degree (*extremely, completely*).

Grammar Topic 6.4
Confusing Words: *We're/Were/Where*

The words *we're, were,* and *where* sound similar, but they are used very differently. Do not confuse them in your writing.

we're	= contraction (*we are*)	**We're** planning to return these books to the library today.
were	= simple past of *be*	The boxes **were** empty when we found them.
where	= a place	No one knows **where** the court trial will take place.

ACTIVITY 13 Working with Confusing Words: *We're/Were/Where*

Complete each of the following sentences with we're, were, *or* where.

1. _____ ready to take the children to the cinema, but we do not know _____ it is located.

2. The police want to know _____ the men _____ last night.

3. I do not know why you could not find us this morning. Sheila and I _____ _____ we told you that we would be waiting for you.

4. We have to hurry. If _____ late again, we are going to be fired.

5. Most of the discussions _____ about the place _____ next year's meeting will take place.

Grammar Topic 6.5
Word Parts

You can increase your vocabulary in two basic ways. One is to learn words that you have never seen before. The second is to learn word parts, which will help you to understand how other words are constructed. Recognizing word parts and using them correctly will increase your vocabulary and thus improve your writing.

NOTE: See the Brief Writer's Handbook with Activities, pages 192–193, for more information on word parts.

Read the paragraph. Eight of the eleven underlined words contain an error with word parts. Correct the error or write C (correct).

The United Farm Workers Union

In the 1950's, Mexican-American farmers began a long fight for (1.) fairness

_____ working conditions in the (2.) agriculturally _____ industry

in the U.S. (3.) Farming _____ was one of the country's largest businesses. Its

(4.) succeed _____ was due, in large part, to (5.) farmer _____

workers. However, the workers were (6.) giving _____ poor housing and (7.) paid

_____ low wages. It was clear that the farm (8.) works _____

needed a labor union, an (9.) organization _____ that would protect and

(10.) defense _____ them. Dolores Huerta and Cesar Chavez worked together

to create a union that would later be (11.) call _____ the United Farm Workers.

Seven of the ten sentences contain an error involving one of the grammar topics featured in this unit. Write a C before the three correct sentences. Write X before the incorrect sentences, circle the error, and write a correction above it.

_____ 1. When the schoolchildren visited the museum, their teacher advised him to be careful.

_____ 2. Do you know where we're going?

_____ 3. When we were in Mexico City last year, we had seen the famous Aztec pyramids there.

_____ 4. Ernesto graduated from high school at the top of his class and then announced he would spend three months doing volunteer work in a foreign country his parents had never heard of, which worried them tremendously.

_____ 5. The committee members recommended enacting a law requiring that drivers wear seatbelts when operating a vehicle, and they were delighted.

_____ 6. When he saw that his cat has dropped a half-eaten rat by the door, Paul flinched.

_____ 7. We're going to the store to pick up groceries for our picnic.

_____ 8. Josh is always so happy, especially when he dances wild with his friends.

_____ 9. Coordinating their efforts took a lot of time, but they were delighted when all of their work has paid off.

_____ 10. Ping-pong might not seem like the most challenging or taxing of sports, but the athletes who play the game know better.

Seven of the ten underlined words in this paragraph contain an error involving one of the grammar topics featured in this unit. Correct the errors on the lines provided. If the word or phrase is correct, write C.

EXAMPLE PARAGRAPHS

Frequent Flyer Miles

When employees fly for their jobs, who should receive the frequent flyer points and free trips that they earn on that airline—the employees or the company? In a (1.) <u>recently</u> _____ meeting, Diana, Jean, and Larry (2.) <u>analyzed</u> _____ the quarterly expense report. "Look at line 415," Diana said.

"Air-travel expenses (3.) <u>had increased</u> _____ 28 percent from last year. Is there any room for savings there?"

"Jean and I were discussing that earlier," Larry said. "I think we should begin (4.) <u>requirement</u> _____ our people to join all the frequent-flyer programs so that after they fly 20,000 to 30,000 miles on any one airline, they get a free ticket. Then we should require them to use that free ticket the next time (5.) <u>they</u> _____ have to take a business trip for us."

"I disagree," Jean said. "To begin with, there is no easy way to enforce the (6.) <u>require</u> _____. Who is going to keep track of (7.) <u>exact</u> _____ where each person goes, how many miles each person flies on each airline, and when a free flight coupon is due to that person? It would make us (8.) <u>appear</u> _____ to be **Big Brother**, looking over their shoulders all the time."

Diana put an end to the discussion. "Both of you think about the matter some more and let me have a memo by next week giving me your position. Then I (9.) <u>decide</u> _____. It is important that (10.) <u>were</u> _____ considering all possible options here."

Big Brother: a phrase describing a government that controls the lives of its citizens

For more practice with the grammar topics from the unit, try Unit 6, Activity 4 on the *Great Writing 5* Web site: elt.heinle.com/greatwriting

ACTIVITY 17 Word Associations

Circle the word or phrase that is most closely related to the word or phrase on the left. If necessary, use a dictionary to check the meaning of words you do not know.

1.	a liability	a problem	an advantage
2.	intertwined	wrapped together	remembered many details
3.	ethnic	groups of people	groups of animals
4.	cultural	plants	people
5.	background	heritage	future
6.	paternal	related to one's father	related to one's mother
7.	maternal	related to one's father	related to one's mother
8.	to translate	to maintain	to change
9.	constantly	sometimes	always
10.	to interpret	to translate	to underestimate
11.	a situation	a quiz	a predicament
12.	a boiling point	a climax	a tragedy
13.	blocks	neighborhoods	neighbors
14.	monolingual	one language	many languages
15.	a handicap	an asset	a disability
16.	potentially	gradually	possibly
17.	in a row	consecutively	unusually
18.	bilingual	two languages	two situations
19.	to enable	to make difficult	to make possible
20.	redundant	unnecessary	compulsory

Fill in each blank with the word or phrase on the left that most naturally completes the phrase on the right. If necessary, use a dictionary to check the meaning of words you do not know.

1. speak / do not speak   I _____ a word of Japanese

2. down / over   to live _____ the street

3. up / on   to pick me _____

4. reach / take   to _____ a boiling point

5. into / above   to turn _____

6. to people / people to   it enables _____

7. of / for   instead _____

8. other / another   to each _____

9. from / over   originally _____ England

10. in / sometimes   grew up _____

11. cultural / quiet   a _____ neighborhood

12. for / of   the importance _____ something

13. of / to   to not speak a word _____ Spanish

14. enable / gather   to _____ data

15. from / without   a few blocks _____ our house

16. up / over   ended _____ in the wrong neighborhood

17. from / of   to get help _____ the police

18. dangerous / translated   potentially _____

19. with / of   to help us _____

20. comments / fragments   to elicit _____

Original Student Writing: Narrative Essay

In this section, you will follow the seven steps in the writing process to write a narrative essay. To review the details of each step, see Unit 1, pages 7–13.

Using the seven steps that follow, write a narrative essay.

Step 1: Choose a Topic

Your first step is to choose a topic for your essay. Choose a story about your life that you want to share with readers. Your teacher may assign a topic, you may think of one yourself, or you may choose one from the suggestions below. As you consider possible topics, ask yourself, "Would readers be interested in this story? If so, why? What exactly would readers like to know?" (Remember that you are interested in the story because it happened to you, but consider your story from another person's point of view. Is it really an interesting story?)

Humanities	Write a narrative essay describing what experiences led you to choose your college major.
Sciences	Describe your most interesting experience with science and explain why you enjoy studying science.
Business	Describe your experiences in the business world. Did you have a part-time or full-time job that encouraged you to major in business in college? Explain how your life experiences have led you to major in business.
Personal	What is the biggest, most embarrassing mistake you made in your life? What did you learn from this experience?

1. What topic did you choose? _____

2. Why did you choose this topic? _____

   _____

   _____

   _____

Step 2: Brainstorm

Use this space to jot down as many ideas about the topic as you can.

Brainstorming Box

Step 3: Outline

Prepare a simple outline of your essay. Use the following outline or the outline of narrative elements on the next page.

Title: _____

I. Introduction

    A. Hook: _____

    _____

    B. Connecting information: _____

    _____

    _____

    C. Thesis statement: _____

    _____

II. Body Paragraph 1 (Point 1): _____

    A. _____

    B. _____

III. Body Paragraph 2 (Point 2): _____

    A. _____

    B. _____

IV. Body Paragraph 3 (Point 3): _____

    A. _____

    B. _____

V. Conclusion: _____

    _____

    _____

Outline of narrative elements

Setting: _____

_____

Main Characters: _____

_____

Plot: _____

_____

Climax: _____

_____

Ending: _____

_____

Peer Editing of Outlines

Exchange books with a partner. Read your partner's outline. Then use the following questions to help you to comment on your partner's outline. Use your partner's feedback to revise your outline.

1. Is there any aspect of the outline that looks unclear to you?

_____

_____

_____

2. Can you think of an area in the outline that needs more development? Do you have any specific suggestions?

_____

_____

_____

3. If you have any other ideas or suggestions, write them here.

_____

_____

_____

Step 4: Write the First Draft

Use the information from Steps 1, 2, and 3 to write the first draft of your narrative essay. Use at least five of the vocabulary words or phrases presented in Activity 17 and Activity 18. Underline these words and phrases in your essay.

Step 5: Get Feedback from a Peer

Exchange papers from Step 4 with a partner. Read your partner's writing. Then use Peer Editing Sheet 6 on page 219 to help you to comment on your partner's writing. Be sure to offer positive suggestions and comments that will help your partner improve his or her writing.

Step 6: Revise the First Draft

Read the comments on Peer Editing Sheet 6 about your essay. Then reread your essay. Can you identify places where you plan to make revisions? List the improvements you are going to make.

1. _____

_____

_____

2. _____

_____

_____

3. _____

_____

_____

Use all the information from the previous steps to write the final version of your paper. Often, writers will need to write a third or even fourth draft to express their ideas as clearly as possible. Write as many drafts as necessary to produce a good essay.

Step 7: Proofread the Final Draft

Be sure to proofread your paper several times before you submit it.

Additional Topics for Writing

Here are ten topics for additional narrative essay writing.

TOPIC 1: Describe your first trip to the dentist, doctor, or hospital.

TOPIC 2: Describe your last day of high school.

TOPIC 3: Describe your adventures on a trip.

TOPIC 4: Describe a day when something unusual happened where you work.

TOPIC 5: Describe the day when a best friend moved away.

TOPIC 6: Describe a situation when your parents punished you.

TOPIC 7: Describe your proudest moment.

TOPIC 8: Describe a time when you ended a relationship.

TOPIC 9: Describe your most embarrassing moment.

TOPIC 10: Describe a time when you apologized for your actions.

Timed Writing

How quickly can you write in English? There are many times when you must write quickly, such as on a test. It is important to feel comfortable during those times. Timed-writing practice can make you feel better about writing quickly in English.

First, read the essay guidelines below. Then take out a piece of paper. Read the writing prompt below the guidelines. As quickly as you can, write a basic outline for this writing prompt (including the thesis and your three main points). You should spend <u>no more than</u> 5 minutes on your outline.

You will then have 40 minutes to write a 5-paragraph narrative essay about your topic. At the end of the 40 minutes, your teacher will collect your work and return it to you at a later date.

Narrative Essay Guidelines

- Remember to give your essay a title.

- Double-space your essay.

- Write as legibly as possible (if you are not using a computer).

- Include a short introduction (with a thesis statement), three body paragraphs, and a conclusion.

- Most narratives tell a story from the past, so double check all of your verbs to make sure they match the time of your events.

- Try to give yourself a few minutes before the end of the activity to review your work. Check for spelling, verb tense, and subject-verb agreement mistakes.

Write an essay describing how you became interested in your favorite hobby.

Brief Writer's Handbook with Activities

Sentence Types

Many writers do not write well because they do not use a variety of types of sentences. In this section, we offer ideas for writing correct sentences of several kinds. This section reviews three sentence types: **simple, compound,** and **complex.** Good writers use all three types of sentences for a variety of styles.

The Two Basic Parts of a Sentence

A sentence in English consists of two parts: **subject** and **predicate.** The subject is the part of the sentence that contains who or what the sentence is about. The predicate contains the verb that tells something about the subject.

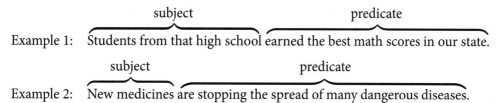

Example 1:   subject: Students from that high school   predicate: earned the best math scores in our state.

Example 2:   subject: New medicines   predicate: are stopping the spread of many dangerous diseases.

The most important part of the predicate is the **verb**, and the most important part of the subject is the **simple subject**. It is often much easier to find the verb first and then to find the subject. In Example 1, the verb is *earned*. The complete subject is *students from that high school*, but can you find one word that is the central idea of the complete subject? In this case, the simple subject is *students*.

In Example 2, the verb is *are stopping*. The complete subject is *new medicines*. The simple subject is *medicines*.

Activity 1 Subjects and Predicates
Read each sentence. Then draw a line between the complete subject and the complete predicate. The first one has been done for you.

1. Many inventions and discoveries | have changed human life forever.

2. In 1875, Alexander Graham Bell made the first telephone, a revolutionary invention for communication.

3. At the young age of 29, Alexander Graham Bell invented the telephone.

4. In the late nineteenth century, Karl Benz designed the first practical automobile with an internal-combustion engine.

5. Barthelemy Thimonnier, a French tailor, invented the world's first sewing machine in 1830.

6. In 1809, Humphry Davy, an English chemist, developed the first electric light.

7. Less than a century ago, Alexander Fleming discovered penicillin.

8. It is impossible to imagine life without these tremendous additions.

Clauses

A **clause** is a subject-verb combination. Study the following examples. The subjects are underlined, and the verbs are **boldfaced**.

Each of the following sentences has one subject-verb combination and therefore one clause:

The girls **played** tennis.

The girls and boys **played** tennis.

The girls and boys **played** tennis and then **went** to the mall.

Each of the following sentences has two subject-verb combinations and therefore two clauses:

The girls **played** tennis, and the boys **went** to the mall.

The girls and boys **played** tennis, and then they **went** to the mall.

NOTE: Sometimes one clause can be inside another clause.

The girls who **played** tennis **went** to the mall later.

There are two kinds of clauses: **independent** and **dependent.**

Independent Clauses

An **independent clause** is easy to recognize because it can stand alone. It has meaning all by itself. Study the following examples. The subjects are underlined, and the verbs are **boldfaced**.

Each of the following sentences has one independent clause:

The girls **played** tennis.

The girls and boys **played** tennis.

The girls and boys **played** tennis and then **went** to the mall.

Each of the following sentences has two independent clauses:

The girls **played** tennis, and the boys **went** to the mall.

The girls and boys **played** tennis, and then they **went** to the mall.

Dependent Clauses

In the sentence below, there are also two clauses, but only one is an independent clause:

The girls who **played** tennis **went** to the mall later.

In this sentence, *The girls . . . went to the mall later* is an independent clause. The words *who played tennis* also make up a clause but cannot stand alone. This clause has no meaning without the rest of the sentence. We call this kind of clause a **dependent clause** because it depends on the rest of the sentence to have meaning.

The dependent clauses in these sentences have been underlined:

The book that I bought is extremely interesting.

A bilingual dictionary is ideal for learners whose English is not good yet.

Activity 2 Independent and Dependent Clauses

Read these six sentences about reality television programs. Identify the underlined clauses as either independent (I) or dependent (D).

_____ 1. Reality television programs, <u>which are quite popular</u>, drive my mother crazy.

_____ 2. *Survivor*, <u>which is broadcast on CBS</u>, places castaways in a remote location and makes them fend for themselves.

_____ 3. *American Idol* <u>is a singing competition</u> that looks for the next vocal superstar.

_____ 4. Many of the singers <u>who audition for *American Idol*</u> are not very talented.

_____ 5. <u>Donald Trump's show *The Apprentice*</u>, in which he hires an intern, <u>is known for its trademark phrase "You're fired."</u>

_____ 6. Jasper is a producer for *Big Brother*, <u>which is much more popular in Britain than in the United States</u>.

Activity 3 Independent and Dependent Clauses

Read these six sentences about Mark Twain. Identify the underlined clauses as either independent (I) or dependent (D).

_____ 1. When Mark Twain was a boy, <u>his family moved to Hannibal, Missouri</u>, where he spent many hours playing on the Mississippi River.

_____ 2. *A Connecticut Yankee in King Arthur's Court*, <u>which is one of Twain's most popular books</u>, was recently made into a movie.

_____ 3. One of Mark Twain's most famous books is *Huckleberry Finn*, <u>which is a story about a young boy and a slave</u>.

_____ 4. <u>Tom Sawyer</u>, whose adventures have delighted many readers, <u>is known for his pluck and determination</u>.

_____ 5. <u>Twain's *Life on the Mississippi* describes adventures</u> that befell him as a riverboat pilot.

_____ 6. Mark Twain was born in 1835 and died in 1910, <u>which were both years when Halley's Comet was in view</u>.

Sentence Type 1: Simple Sentences

A **simple sentence** has one subject-verb combination.

> <u>I</u> **have** a cat.
>
> <u>My cat</u> **is** gray.
>
> <u>The name of my cat</u> **begins** with the letter *B*.

A simple sentence can have two or more subjects.

> <u>France</u> and <u>Germany</u> **are** located in Europe.
>
> Because of the heavy rains yesterday, <u>Highway 50</u>, <u>Eisenhower Boulevard</u>, and <u>Temple Avenue</u> **were** impassable.

A simple sentence can have two or more verbs.

> The <u>cat</u> **curled up** into a ball and **went** to sleep.
>
> The <u>cat</u> **yawned**, **curled up** into a ball, and **went** to sleep.

Activity 4 Subjects and Verbs

Read these sentences about Saturday Night Live. *Underline the subject and circle the verb.*

1. A weekly late-night TV show, *Saturday Night Live (SNL)* made its debut on October 11, 1975.

2. Extremely popular in the United States, *Saturday Night Live* has launched the careers of many famous comedians, including John Belushi, Eddie Murphy, and Mike Meyers.

3. Lorne Michaels, a Canadian, has produced and managed *SNL* for more than 25 years.

4. The weekly guest host of *SNL* plays an active role in picking the skits for the show.

5. At the precocious age of seven, Drew Barrymore hosted *SNL*.

Sentence Type 2: Compound Sentences

A **compound sentence** has two or more subject-verb combinations.

> The <u>rain</u> **began** to fall, so <u>we</u> **stopped** playing tennis.
>
> The <u>store</u> **had** a special sale on children's clothes, and <u>hundreds</u> of parents **flocked** there to shop for bargains.

In a compound sentence, the subject-verb combinations are connected by a **coordinating conjunction**. To remember coordinating conjunctions, you can use the mnemonic *FANBOYS* (*for, and, nor, but, or, yet, so*). Of these seven coordinating conjunctions, the most commonly used are *and*, *but*, and *so*.

for:	<u>I</u> **will not tell** a lie, *for* <u>it</u> **would not be** honest.
and:	<u>Helen</u> **takes** the car, *and* <u>she</u> **picks up** Larry on the way to work.
nor:	<u>I</u> **would not like** to join you for lunch, *nor* **would** <u>I</u> **like** to join you for dinner.
but:	<u>Carrie</u> **wanted** to go to the disco, *but* <u>Francis</u> **refused** to join her there.
or:	**Do** <u>I</u> **want** to go now, *or* **do** <u>I</u> **want** to go later?
yet:	University <u>students</u> often **take** an overload of courses, *yet* <u>they</u> **should know** not to overtax themselves.
so:	The <u>teacher</u> **prepared** her courses the night before, *so* <u>she</u> **was** ready for everything that happened the following day.

Activity 5 Simple and Compound Sentences

Read these eight sentences about the Super Bowl. Identify each sentence as simple (S) or compound (C). In the compound sentences, circle the coordinating conjunction.

_____ 1. The Super Bowl is one of the biggest sporting events of the year, so it is always one of the most watched television shows of the year.

_____ 2. The Pittsburgh Steelers, the Dallas Cowboys, and the San Francisco Forty-Niners have each won four or more Super Bowls.

_____ 3. Many millions of people watch the Super Bowl on television, and many companies therefore spend millions of dollars advertising their products during the show.

_____ 4. One of the most famous commercials ever shown during the Super Bowl was a commercial modeled on George Orwell's book *1984*.

_____ 5. The Buffalo Bills lost four Super Bowls in a row, and this accomplishment makes them one of the saddest footnotes in Super Bowl history.

_____ 6. New Orleans, Jacksonville, and Houston have all hosted the Super Bowl, which brings in millions of dollars to the economies of these locales.

_____ 7. Other major sporting events include the Stanley Cup for hockey, Wimbledon for tennis, and the World Series for baseball.

_____ 8. Many people would like to attend the championship games of major sporting teams, but the tickets are quite expensive.

Activity 6 Identifying Compound Sentences

Read these sentences about the great writer Geoffrey Chaucer. Underline the two compound sentences.

EXAMPLE PARAGRAPH

Chaucer is quite possibly the greatest writer of English literature. He was most likely born in the early 1340s, and he died in 1400. Relatively little is known about his early life. He came from a well-to-do merchant family that had lived for several generations in Ipswich, some 70 miles northeast of London. No school records of Chaucer have survived. The earliest known document that bears the name of Geoffrey Chaucer is a fragmentary household account book dated between 1356 and 1359. Chaucer is best known for his collection of stories called the *Canterbury Tales*, but this collection of stories is unfinished.

Activity 7 Identifying Compound Sentences

Read this paragraph from an essay in Unit 6. Underline the two compound sentences.

Coming from a multilingual family sparked many difficulties in communication. For example, when my maternal grandparents would fly from North America to South America to visit us, my mother had to translate among the different family members. We spoke Spanish in our house, but my American grandparents spoke only English. Since they did not speak a word of Spanish, my mother was constantly interpreting questions and answers. Rather than enjoying their visit, my mother had to work as a translator. With my mom's help, I could understand my grandparents, but I wanted to be able to speak to them by myself.

Activity 8 Original Compound Sentences

Write five compound sentences. Use a different coordinating conjunction in each one.

1. _____

   _____

2. _____

   _____

3. _____

   _____

4. _____

   _____

5. _____

   _____

Sentence Type 3: Complex Sentences

A **complex sentence** has at least one independent clause and one dependent clause. Dependent clauses may begin with a variety of connector words. Adverb clauses often begin with words such as *after, because,* or *although.* Noun clauses may begin with *who, what, why,* or *that.* Adjective clauses frequently begin with *that, which,* or *who.*

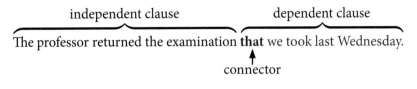

independent clause   dependent clause

The professor returned the examination **that** we took last Wednesday.

↑
connector

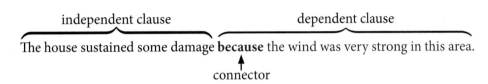

independent clause   dependent clause

The house sustained some damage **because** the wind was very strong in this area.

↑
connector

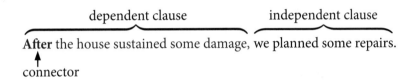

dependent clause   independent clause

After the house sustained some damage, we planned some repairs.

↑
connector

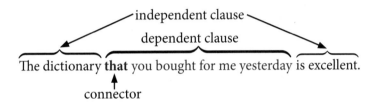

independent clause

dependent clause

The dictionary **that** you bought for me yesterday is excellent.

↑
connector

Activity 9 Identifying Independent and Dependent Clauses

Read the following eight sentences about inventions. Each one is a complex sentence. Draw two lines under the independent clause and one line under the dependent clause. The first one has been done for you.

1. The electric light bulb that we depend on every night for light was invented in 1900.

2. Because the Internet is useful and practical, it has caught on rapidly with all ages.

3. Although people complain about high gas prices, no one has invented a fuel-free vehicle yet.

4. Do you know the name of the person who invented the radio?

5. One of the most important inventions that we use every day without thinking has to be the simple ink pen.

6. When electricity was invented, many people were afraid to have it in their houses.

7. How did people in warm climates survive before air-conditioning was invented?

8. When portable media players were introduced, they quickly revolutionized the music industry.

Sentence Variety: Adding Adjectives

Adding adjectives to sentences is one of the best ways to improve sentences. Adjectives can add color and vigor to otherwise dull sentences. Adjectives are usually placed in front of nouns.

Good: The wind blew across the lake.

Better: The **cold** wind blew across the **frozen** lake.

Activity 10 Original Writing with Adjectives

Add adjectives on the lines in the paragraph to improve this story.

Once upon a time, there was a/an _____ monster that lived in a/an

_____ forest. The monster was _____. One day, the monster met

a/an _____ frog. When the monster asked the frog whether he was ugly, the frog

replied, "You are not ugly. You are _____." The monster and frog then became

friends and soon met a/an _____ princess. Since the princess was

_____, she immediately told them that they were both _____.

The _____ monster, _____ frog, and _____

princess soon became _____ allies.

Activity 11 Order of Adjectives

Read the following paragraph about persuasive writing. Write the words below in the correct order on the lines in the paragraph.

1. effective writing persuasive
2. people other
3. view our point unique of
4. set exercises next the of
5. brief a essay
6. given a subject

Much of the writing that we do is persuasive. In (1.) _____

_____, we encourage (2.) _____ to see (3.) _____

_____. In the sample essay, the writer wants to convince the reader that

spam should be outlawed. Through (4.) _____, you will

go through the process of writing (5.) _____ in which you try

to persuade your reader to agree with you on (6.) _____.

Activity 12 Order of Adjectives

Read the following paragraph about the composer Franz Schubert. Write the words below in the correct order on the lines in the paragraph. (NOTE: Some words may already be in the correct order.)

1. the brilliant composers most
2. first composition his
3. his symphony first
4. a prolific composer

5. pieces numerous piano
6. works only few Schubert's a of
7. poverty continuous

EXAMPLE PARAGRAPH

One of (1.) _____ that the world has ever

seen, Franz Schubert (1797–1828), was born in Vienna and lived there until his death. He wrote

(2.) _____ at the age of 13 and wrote

(3.) _____ at the age of 16. Like Mozart, Schubert

was (4.) _____ . His list of 998 extant works

includes seven masses, nine symphonies, (5.) _____ ,

and 606 songs. In a single year, 1815, at the age of 18, he wrote 140 songs. (6.) _____

_____ were published in his lifetime. Nor did he profit much from those

that he did sell. Like Mozart, he suffered from (7.) _____ .

Activity 13 Adjectives in Real-World Sentences

Copy five sentences from a novel, a magazine, a newspaper, or the Internet. Circle all the adjectives.

1. _____

_____

2. _____

_____

3. _____

_____

4. _____

_____

5. _____

_____

Activity 14 Adding Adjectives to Improve Sentences

Write five sentences without adjectives. Then write the same sentences with adjectives. For variety, add at least two adjectives to some of your new sentences.

1. Original Sentence: _____

   Improved Sentence: _____

   _____

2. Original Sentence: _____

   Improved Sentence: _____

   _____

3. Original Sentence: _____

   Improved Sentence: _____

   _____

4. Original Sentence: _____

   Improved Sentence: _____

   _____

5. Original Sentence: _____

   Improved Sentence: _____

   _____

Prepositional Phrases

Another easy way to add variety to your sentences is to add **prepositional phrases.** A prepositional phrase consists of a preposition and an object (a noun or a pronoun). Study these examples:

> A new ambassador **to** a foreign country must learn the customs **of** this country quite quickly.

> When I first got an e-mail account ten years ago, I received communications only **from** friends, family, and professional acquaintances.

Notice that the next example has eighteen words, but only four of the words are not part of a prepositional phrase:

> **With** the advent **of** electricity **in** the late nineteenth century, thousands **of** people advanced their quality **of** life.

Prepositional phrases can serve all sorts of purposes. For example, prepositional phrases can tell *where* (in the kitchen), *when* (in the late seventeenth century), and *why* (for a better life).

Perhaps the most commonly used prepositions are *at, on, in, for, before, after, with,* and *without.* Here is a larger list:

Prepositions			
about	besides	in lieu of	regarding
above	between	in spite of	since
according to	beyond	including	through
across	by	inside	throughout
after	concerning	instead of	till
against	contrary to	into	to
ahead of	despite	like	toward
along	down	near	under
among	due to	next to	underneath
around	during	of	until
at	except	off	up
because of	for	on	upon
before	from	on account of	versus
behind	in	out	via
below	in addition to	outside	with
beneath	in back of	over	within
beside	in front of	past	without

Activity 15 Identifying Prepositional Phrases

Read these paragraphs about a famous landmark in California. Underline the prepositional phrases and draw a circle around the prepositions.

EXAMPLE PARAGRAPHS

Millions of people all over the world have seen the Golden Gate Bridge in San Francisco, so people now equate the Golden Gate Bridge with the city of San Francisco. Although they know that the Golden Gate Bridge is in San Francisco, what they do not know is that the nickname of this structure was "the bridge that couldn't be built." The idea of the construction of a bridge across San Francisco Bay had been discussed for years before the construction of the Golden Gate Bridge was actually started in 1933. For a variety of reasons, this bridge was long considered impossible to build.

First of all, the weather in the area—with high winds, rain, and fog—was rarely good. Second, engineers thought that the strong ocean currents in the bay meant that the bridge could not be built. Furthermore, they were worried about how the strong winds in the area would affect any large structure. Finally, it was the Depression. The poor economy was causing people to experience incredible difficulties, so many people thought that it would be foolish to spend such a large amount of money on such an impossible project.

Sentence Problems: Fragments, Run-ons, Comma Splices

Three common sentence problems are fragments, run-ons, and comma splices.

What Is a Fragment?

A **fragment** is an incomplete sentence.

> Running as fast as he can.
>
> The house at the end of the block.
>
> To make a medical breakthrough.

All complete sentences must contain a **subject** and a **verb**. The fragments above can be turned into complete sentences rather easily.

> <u>He</u> **is running** as fast as he can.
>
> The <u>house</u> at the end of the block **belongs** to the Meyers.
>
> The <u>research teams</u> **hope** to make a medical breakthrough.

Sometimes fragments contain a **subject** and a **verb,** but they are dependent clauses. When a fragment is incorrectly separated from an independent clause, either the dependent clause must be made into a complete sentence or the dependent clause must be attached to an independent clause.

Fragment (dependent clause):	Because I studied so hard last night.
Independent clause:	I studied so hard last night.
Combined clauses:	Because I studied so hard last night, I easily passed my exam.
Fragment (dependent clause):	After the rain started.
Independent clause:	The rain started.
Combined clauses:	After the rain started, the roads became slippery.

Activity 1 Identifying Fragments

Identify each item below as a sentence (S) *or a fragment* (F).

1. _____ Jason went to the store and bought onions.

   _____ Not realizing at the time that he needed ginger as well.

2. _____ Making her decision carefully.

   _____ Pamela ordered two cups of coffee.

   _____ Hoping her friend would arrive on time.

3. _____ We will first take the children to the zoo, and then we will go to dinner.

4. _____ As summer vacation comes closer, I find myself planning a trip to the Caribbean.

   _____ To think about this makes me happy.

5. _____ I cannot believe what Sheila did, and I am not happy about it!

6. _____ I still love my old pony.

   _____ Although it does not run that fast.

7. _____ With my father nearby, I reached for the broom.

   _____ Leaning over too far caused me to fall.

8. _____ They were all having a good time.

   _____ Even the grown-ups.

Activity 2 Correcting Fragments

Rewrite the five fragments from Activity 1 so that they are complete sentences.

a. _____

   _____

b. _____

   _____

c. _____

   _____

d. _____

   _____

e. _____

   _____

Activity 3 Identifying and Correcting Fragments

Read this paragraph. Underline the one fragment. On the lines below the paragraph, rewrite the fragment to make it a complete sentence.

The café plays an important role in the daily life of French people. Students go there at any time of day not only to have something to eat or drink but also to relax, to read the paper, or to listen to music. Since many students live quite a distance from the university and since the existing libraries are often overcrowded. The café also offers a place to study. For many young people, the café is the ideal spot to meet one's friends or to strike up a casual conversation with other students. Most French cafés are divided into two parts: the inside section and the terrace, which extends onto the sidewalk. In spring and summer, most customers prefer the terrace, where they can enjoy the good weather and observe the people walking by.

_____

_____

Activity 4 Identifying and Correcting Fragments

Read this paragraph. Underline the two fragments. On the lines below the paragraph, rewrite the fragments to make them complete sentences.

I read two books on business communication. The first book, *Effective Business Communication,* is an essential resource on business correspondence for the modern office. In today's business climate, revolutionized by electronic mail and overnight package delivery. It is important to communicate clearly and precisely in writing. *Effective Business Communication* offers sound advice for business writers; it is comprehensive yet concise. The second book is *Business Writing for Today.* Also claims to be an essential source on business correspondence for today's business world. However, this book is not as well-written or as comprehensive. *Business Writing for Today* discusses a few aspects of e-mail that are not covered in *Effective Business Communication.* The authors then move on to samples of business correspondence, but these samples lack any information about the senders' reasons for writing these letters. Therefore, it is my opinion that *Effective Business Communication* would certainly be a more valuable resource guide to have in the office than *Business Writing for Today.*

1. _____

_____

_____

2. _____

_____

_____

Activity 5 Identifying and Correcting Fragments

Read this paragraph. Underline the two fragments. On the lines below the paragraph, rewrite the fragments to make them complete sentences.

EXAMPLE PARAGRAPH

French is widely spoken in Africa. The use of French as a common language is a factor of national integration and cohesion. Where different ethnic groups have traditionally spoken different languages. Twenty African countries use French as their official language. Among the most important French-speaking countries in Africa are Madagascar, Zaire, Senegal, Mali, and Ivory Coast. Formerly French or Belgian colonies. These countries became independent nations in the early 1960s. French is also spoken by large segments of the population in the northern African countries of Morocco, Algeria, and Tunisia.

1. _____

_____

_____

2. _____

_____

_____

Activity 6 Identifying and Correcting Fragments

Read this paragraph. Underline the two fragments. On the lines below the paragraph, rewrite the fragments to make them complete sentences.

Chaucer was likely born in the early 1340s and died in 1400. Is quite possibly the greatest writer of English literature. Relatively little is known about his early life. He came from a well-to-do merchant family that lived for several generations in Ipswich, some 70 miles northeast of London. No school records of Chaucer have survived. The earliest known document that names Geoffrey Chaucer is a fragmentary household account book. Dated between 1356 and 1359. Chaucer is best known for his collection of stories called the *Canterbury Tales,* but this collection of stories is unfinished.

1. _____

_____

_____

2. _____

_____

_____

What Is a Run-on?

A **run-on sentence** is an error in which a sentence lacks the necessary structure to link its ideas together. Typically, a run-on sentence contains two independent clauses incorrectly linked to each another. You might think of a run-on sentence as a wreck in which two sentences crash together.

Activity 7 Identifying Run-on Problems

Identify each of these sentences as a run-on sentence (RO) or a complete sentence (CS).

_____ 1. Sheryl always told me not to trust a salesperson like that if only I had listened to her everything would have been fine.

_____ 2. It takes a long time to knit someone a sweater, but it is a wonderful feeling to give someone a gift that is truly a labor of love.

_____ 3. The Roman troops in England faced many almost insurmountable difficulties, including disease, hunger, and learning about the new environment.

_____ 4. The cat gets hungry around 3 P.M. make sure you are there to feed it.

_____ 5. It is amazing to me that I still watch such childish TV shows as I did when I was a kid, but I really do enjoy them.

_____ 6. Chaucer is known as the "Father of the English Language" he wrote the *Canterbury Tales*.

_____ 7. The capital city of Malaysia is Kuala Lumpur, but the seat of the nation's government is in Putrajaya.

_____ 8. We cannot get a taxi because of the rain if we cannot get a taxi we will miss our plane.

Activity 8 Correcting Run-on Problems

Rewrite the four run-on sentences from Activity 7 so that they are correct sentences.

a. _____

_____

b. _____

_____

c. _____

_____

d. _____

_____

Activity 9 Identifying and Correcting Run-on Problems

Read this paragraph about a well-known author. Underline the two run-ons. On the lines below the paragraph, rewrite the sentences so that they are correct.

EXAMPLE PARAGRAPH

Carson McCullers left behind an impressive literary legacy, she died at the age of 50 in 1967. Her work included five novels, two plays, 20 short stories, some two dozen nonfiction pieces, a book of children's verse, and a handful of distinguished poems. Her most acclaimed fiction appeared in the 1940s. McCullers was taken for an exceptional writer at the age of just 23. That was when she published *The Heart Is a Lonely Hunter* (1940), which is set in a small Southern mill town resembling Columbus, Georgia, where she was born on February 19, 1917. People loved this novel, the novel accurately reflects the author's culture and is her most autobiographical tale.

1. _____

_____

2. _____

_____

What Is a Comma Splice?

A **comma splice** is a special kind of run-on sentence in which two independent clauses are joined by a comma. Unfortunately, a comma is not strong enough for this task. Independent clauses must be joined by a semicolon or by a comma and a conjunction.

Activity 10 Identifying Comma Splice Problems

Identify each as a sentence (S) or a comma splice (CS).

_____ 1. It is really hot outside today, let's go swimming.

_____ 2. Patsy asked me to join her, and I said that I would.

_____ 3. The jury returned a guilty verdict; the defendant sobbed.

_____ 4. On that TV program, Jack Wallace is Chuck Smith's next door neighbor, this show is about how Jack annoys Chuck all the time.

_____ 5. Cell phones are becoming increasingly popular, and land lines will likely become less and less popular.

_____ 6. My little sister is always cajoling me to help her with her homework, but I encourage her to do it on her own.

_____ 7. My friend Harry will never go to a movie by himself, I go to movies by myself all the time.

_____ 8. I enjoy cooking a lot, seafood is my favorite cuisine.

Activity 11 Correcting Comma Splice Problems

Rewrite the four comma splices from Activity 10 so that they are correct sentences.

a. _____

_____

b. _____

_____

c. _____

_____

d. _____

_____

Preposition Combinations

Verb + Preposition Combinations

Verb + Preposition			
account for	complain about	hope for	stop from
agree on	comply with	listen to	substitute for
agree with	consist of	look at	talk to
apply for	count on	look for	think about
approve of	depend on	pay for	think of
belong to	hear about	rely on	wait for
care about	hear from	stare at	work on

Adjective + Preposition Combinations

Adjective + Preposition			
accustomed to	connected to/with	famous for	responsible for
acquainted with	delighted at/about	frustrated with	satisfied with
afraid of	dependent on	guilty of	serious about
answerable to	different from	interested in	similar to
attached to	disappointed with/in/by	opposed to	suitable for
aware of	doubtful about	pleased with	suspicious of
bad at	enthusiastic about	popular with	typical of
bored with	envious of	proud of	used to (= accustomed to)
capable of	excited about	related to	

Noun + Preposition Combinations

Noun + Preposition			
advantage of	demand for	invitation to	price of
application for	difference between	lack of	reason for
benefit of	difficulty with	matter with	reply to
cause of	example of	need for	request for
cost of	increase/decrease in, of	opinion of	solution to
decision to	interest in	order for	trouble with

Word Parts (Suffixes)

Studying word parts will help you figure out the meaning of new words and increase your academic vocabulary.

Adjective Endings

Ending	Meaning	Examples
-able / -ible	able to	likable, flexible
-al	having the quality of	optional, original
-ant	having the quality of	pleasant, resultant
-ar / -ary	related to	muscular, culinary
-ed	past participle	delighted, surprised
-en	made of	golden, wooden
-ent	having the quality of	apparent, insistent
-esque	in the style of	grotesque, picturesque
-ful	full of	careful, mindful
-ing	present participle	amazing, distressing
-ive	tending to	creative, destructive
-less	without	aimless, hopeless
-like	like, similar to	childlike, ladylike
-ly	having the quality of	friendly, manly
-ory	related to	obligatory, sensory
-ous / -ious	full of	famous, religious
-proof	protected from	fireproof, waterproof
-ward	in the direction of	backward, downward
-y	related to	lazy, windy

Noun Endings

Ending	Meaning	Examples
-an / -ian	person related to	American, guardian
-ance / -ence	condition, state	relevance, existence
-ant / -ent	person who	entrant, student
-ation	action, state	imagination, explanation
-ee	person who receives something	lessee, trustee
-er / -or	person who does	baker, sailor
-ese	person related to	Japanese, Taiwanese

Ending	Meaning	Examples
-hood	state of	neighborhood, childhood
-ics	science, art, or practice	physics, statistics
-ing	gerund (action)	dancing, reading
-ion / -sion / -tion	action, state, result	union, conclusion, reaction
-ist	person who believes or does	communist, typist
-ment	result of action	document, placement
-ness	quality, state	friendliness, trustworthiness
-ship	condition, quality	friendship, leadership
-ty / -ity	quality, condition	density, equality

Verb Endings

Ending	Meaning	Examples
-ate	cause, make	calculate, demonstrate
-en	cause to become	fatten, shorten
-ify	make	clarify, terrify
-ize	make	demonize, plagiarize

Adverb Endings

Ending	Meaning	Examples
-ly	manner of	carefully, unequivocally

Examples of Word Forms across Parts of Speech

Noun	Verb	Adjective	Adverb
action	act	active	actively
benefit	benefit	beneficial	beneficially
care	care	careful, caring	carefully, caringly
difference	differ	different	differently
education	educate	educational	educationally
imagination	imagine	imaginative	imaginatively
persuasion	persuade	persuasive	persuasively
temptation	tempt	tempting	temptingly

Additional Grammar Activities

Activity 1 Prepositions
Underline the correct preposition in each set of parentheses.

(1. In / On) 1812, a collection of fairy tales, or folktales, was published. These stories became very popular not only (2. at / in) Germany but also throughout Europe and America. The brothers Jakob and Wilhelm Grimm collected the stories during a period that was characterized (3. by / for) a great interest (4. for / in) German folklore. Whatever the historical background of the stories, they have long been a part (5. in / of) childhood experience. Children identify (6. for / with) the hero, suffer through the inevitable trials and tribulations, and experience relief and triumph when virtue is finally rewarded. Fairy tales are not only (7. for / to) children, however. Today, this fairy-tale society, founded (8. at / in) 1956 in Germany, has more than 600 members from all over Europe. Scholars publish books (9. on / through) fairy-tale motifs and use fairy tales as a source (10. of / on) information (11. about / for) life and values (12. in / on) different times and cultures.

Activity 2 Verb Tenses
Underline the correct verb tense in each set of parentheses.

Carson McCullers left behind an impressive literary legacy when she (1. has died / died) at the age of 50 in 1967: five novels, two plays, 20 short stories, two dozen nonfiction pieces, a book of children's verse, and a handful of distinguished poems. Her most acclaimed fiction (2. appears / appeared) in the 1940s. McCullers was taken for an exceptional writer when she (3. publishes / published) *The Heart Is a Lonely Hunter* (1940) at age 23. This work (4. is / has) set in a small Southern mill town resembling Columbus, Georgia, where she was born Lula Carson Smith on February 19, 1917. The novel (5. reflects / reflected) the author's culture and (6. is / will be) her most autobiographical tale.

Activity 3 Editing for Specific Errors

Find these 12 errors and correct them: word form (4), verb tense (3), subject-verb agreement (1), preposition (2), and article (2).

Johann Wolfgang von Goethe (1749–1832) was universal genius. He was a poem, novelist, dramatist, public administrator, and scientist. He had made significant contributions for the fields of optics, comparative anatomy, and plant morphology. The collected works of this prolific writer appear in sixty volumes before his death. Goethe is one of the greatest lyric poets, and his poetry are read and studied today. Modern theaters present his dramatic. His most famous single work is *Faust*, on which he works his entire lifetime; he published the Part 1 in 1808 and Part 2 in 1832. Early in his career, Goethe was already recognition both in Germany and abroad as one of the great figures of world literary. He can confidently hold his place with the select group from Homer, Dante, and Shakespeare.

Activity 4 Editing for Specific Errors

Find these 5 errors and correct them: subject-verb agreement (2), articles (2), and word form (1).

What is the story behind the origin of the word *asparagus*? This vegetable name have a very bizarre history. The word *asparagus* means "sparrow grass." What possibility connection could there be between a sparrow, which is name of a beautiful little brown bird, and this vegetable? In former times, the people were served asparagus accompanied by cooked sparrows! Because this green, grasslike vegetable were served with little sparrows, it became known as "sparrow grass" or asparagus.

Activity 5 Prepositions

Complete the paragraph with the prepositions from the box below.

among	as	by	in	in	in	of	of

French is widely spoken (1.) _____ Africa. The use (2.) _____ French as a common language is a factor of national integration and cohesion where different ethnic groups have traditionally spoken different languages. Twenty African countries use French (3.) _____ their official language. (4.) _____ the most important French-speaking countries in Africa are Madagascar, Zaire, Senegal, Mali, and Ivory Coast. Formerly French or Belgian colonies, these countries became independent nations (5.) _____ the early 1960s. French is also spoken (6.) _____ large segments of the population (7.) _____ the northern African countries (8.) _____ Morocco, Algeria, and Tunisia.

Activity 6 Prepositions

Underline the correct preposition in each set of parentheses.

Chaucer is quite possibly the greatest writer (1. at / of / on) English literature. Relatively little is known (2. about / by / to) his early life. He came (3. by / from / at) a well-to-do merchant family that had lived (4. at / for / without) several generations in Ipswich, some 70 miles northeast of London. No school records (5. at / by / of) Chaucer have survived. The earliest known document that names Geoffrey Chaucer is a fragmentary household account book dated between 1356 and 1359. Chaucer is best known (6. for / like / since) his collection of stories called the *Canterbury Tales*, but this collection (7. at / of / with) stories is unfinished.

Activity 7 Editing Specific Errors

Five of the eight underlined selections contain errors. Correct the error or write C (correct).

You put ketchup on french fries and other foods all the time, but did you ever stop to ask yourself (1.) where this word did come _____ from? Our English word *ketchup* is from the Chinese word *ke-tsiap*. The Chinese created this great food product in the late seventeenth century. Soon afterward, British explorers (2.) come _____ across ketchup in nearby Malaysia and brought it back to the Western world. Fifty years later, this sauce became popular in the American colonies. Around this time, people realized that tomatoes enhanced (3.) flavor _____ of this sauce, so tomatoes were (4.) routinely added _____ to ketchup, and red became the (5.) normally _____ color for this sauce. Oddly enough, ketchup did not (6.) contains _____ any tomatoes until the 1790s (7.) because there was a mistaken presumption that tomatoes were poisonous! _____ Thus, our English word *ketchup* comes from the Chinese name for their original sauce, which was neither red (8.) nor _____ tomato-based.

Activity 8 Editing Specific Errors

Find these 5 errors and correct them: number (1), verb tense (1), comma splice (1), and preposition (2).

One of the most brilliant composer that the world has ever seen, Franz Schubert (1797–1828), was born in Vienna and lived there until his death. He wrote his first composition in the age of 13 and writes his first symphony at the age of 16. Like Mozart, Schubert was a prolific composer. His list of 998 extant works includes seven masses, nine symphonies, numerous piano pieces, and 606 songs, in a single year, 1815, at the age of 18, he wrote 140 songs. Only a few of Schubert's works were published in his lifetime. He did not profit much from those that he did sell. Like Mozart, he suffered for continuous poverty.

Activity 9 Editing Specific Errors

Five of the eight underlined selections contain errors. Correct the error or write C (correct).

For centuries, (1.) the French universities _____ catered only to the educational needs of the students, and their buildings were exclusively academic ones. As the number of university students increased—(2.) more than _____ sevenfold between 1950 and 1989—student residences were added. (3.) In many part of France, _____ the newer city universities were built (4.) in the suburbs, _____ where land (5.) were less expensive, _____ while the academic buildings remained in the center of town. In Paris, (6.) for the example, _____ the city university (7.) is location _____ several miles from the academic Latin Quarter. This creates a serious transportation problem (8.) for the students, _____ who must commute long distances.

Activity 10 Prepositions

Complete the paragraph with the prepositions from the box below.

as	for	for	in	of	to	to	with

Just as it appears to be, the word *strawberry* is actually a combination (1.) _____ the words *straw* and *berry*. *Straw* here is not the straw you use (2.) _____ drinking; instead, it refers (3.) _____ dried cut grass. Strawberries grow very close (4.) _____ the ground, and farmers put straw around the plants to keep the berries off the ground. Coupled (5.) _____ *berry*, the word *straw* indicated the protective aid so necessary (6.) _____ the successful growth of this fruit. This combination resulted (7.) _____ *straw berry* (two words). Eventually, this came to be written (8.) _____ a single word: *strawberry*.

Citations and Plagiarism

Imagine this situation: You have invited some friends over for dinner. Because you did not have time to make a dessert, you stop at a local bakery and pick up a cake. After dinner, your friends compliment you on the delicious cake you made. How do you respond? Most people would give credit to the person who made the cake: "I'm glad you liked it, but I didn't make it. I bought it at Sunshine Bakery." By clarifying that the cake was not yours, you are rightfully giving the credit to Sunshine Bakery. The same concept holds true in writing.

When you write an essay, you should use your own words for the most part. Sometimes, however, writers want to use ideas that they have read in another piece of writing. For example, writers may want to use a quotation from a famous politician if they are writing an essay about a recent election. In this case, the writer must indicate that the idea or the words came from someone else and give credit to that writer. The action of indicating that a writer's words are not original but rather from another source is called **citing.** In academic writing, it is <u>imperative</u> for a writer to cite all information that is not original.

If writers do not give credit for borrowed ideas or borrowed words, they make a serious error. In fact, it is academic theft, and such stealing of ideas or words cannot be tolerated at all. It is not acceptable to use even a few words from another source without citing the source—the amount of information that you borrow is irrelevant. If you steal one sentence or one paragraph, it is still stealing. Stealing someone else's ideas or words and using them in a piece of writing as if they were the writer's original ideas is called **plagiarism**. In an academic setting, plagiarism is considered a very serious offense. In most schools, there are serious academic consequences for plagiarizing any work. For example, some schools require the paper to receive a score of 0 (zero). Other schools will expel the student permanently. In some instances, schools will take both of the above steps.

Does this mean then that writers cannot use other people's words or ideas? No, not at all. In fact, good writing can be strengthened further by using facts from outside sources or quotes from officials to support key points or ideas, so writers should borrow appropriate information. The key to avoiding plagiarism is to cite the source of the information.

Many students have a difficult time knowing when to use a citation, especially if they believe the information is general knowledge. For example, Hessa, a student from the United Arab Emirates (UAE), is writing an essay about her country. She knows that the UAE is made up of seven emirates. Does she need to cite this information? If Hessa is writing this essay in an English-speaking country where people may not know that there are seven emirates, she needs to cite the information. If, however, the information is common knowledge in Hessa's academic community, she would not have to cite the information. In the end, it is better to cite the information than to risk being accused of plagiarism. Before turning in any piece of writing, it is helpful to mark any information that is not your original writing. For any information that you mark, you need to give credit to the person, organization, or Web site that originally wrote it by citing the sources.

Citing: Using a Direct Quotation or Paraphrasing

When you use material from another source, you have two choices: using a **direct quotation** or **paraphrasing**. If a writer uses the exact words (a direct quotation) from a source, the borrowed words must be placed in quotation marks. If a writer borrows an idea from a source but uses his or her original words to express this idea, the writer has used a method called paraphrasing. Paraphrasing does not require quotation marks because the writer is not using the exact words from the original source. However, whether a writer is using an exact quotation or a paraphrased version, the information is not original and must be cited.

Example of a Direct Quotation

Notice that this paragraph from *Vocabulary Myths* (Folse, 2004) contains a direct quote. When you use a direct quote, you must state the name of the author, the date of the publication, and the page number of the direct quotation.

> One of the first observations that second language learners make in their new language is that they need vocabulary knowledge to function well in that language. How frustrating it is when you want to say something and are stymied because you don't know the word for a simple noun even! In spite of

the obvious importance of vocabulary, most courses and curricula tend to be based on grammar or a combination of grammar and communication strategies rather than vocabulary. As a result, even after taking many courses, learners still lack sufficient vocabulary knowledge. Vocabulary knowledge is critical to any communication. Wilkins (1972) summarizes the situation best with "While without grammar very little can be conveyed, without vocabulary *nothing* can be conveyed" (p. 111).

Example of a Longer Quotation

Notice that this paragraph from *Vocabulary Myths* (Folse, 2004) contains a longer direct quote. In this case, the direct quotation is set off differently than original writing.

As more and more empirical research in second language study is made available and results provide important insight into our questions about vocabulary learning and teaching, the education pendulum is swinging back toward some more "traditional" methods, including those which rely on explicit instruction from the teacher. This in turn begs the question of what kinds of classroom activities, especially vocabulary activities, are effective for L2 learners. Carter and McCarthy (1988) conclude that

> although it suffered neglect for a long time, vocabulary pedagogy has benefited in the last fifteen years or so from theoretical advances in the linguistic lexicon, from psycholinguistic investigations into the mental lexicon, from the communicative trend in teaching, which has brought the learner into focus, and from developments in computers. What is perhaps missing in all this is more knowledge about what happens in classrooms when vocabulary crops up (p. 51).

Example of a Paraphrase

Notice that this paragraph from *Vocabulary Myths* (Folse, 2004) contains a paraphrase, or summary, of a concept from a work written by Eskey in 1988. Instead of using any phrases or sentences from Eskey's work, Folse uses a sentence in the paragraph that summarizes Eskey's work and connects that idea to the current paragraph and audience. When you paraphrase material, you must state the name of the author and the date of the publication.

While lack of vocabulary knowledge is a problem across all skill areas, it is especially apparent in ESL reading. Eskey (1988) found that not being able to recognize the meaning of English words automatically causes students who are good readers in their native language to do excessive guesswork in the second language and that this guessing slows down the process of reading.

Bibliography

In addition to providing information on sources in places where they are used within your writing, you should also list all the works, or sources, of the words and ideas you used in the final **bibliography,** or **list of works cited,** at the end of your paper.

Citation methods vary according to academic professions and fields, so you should ask your instructor about the citation system that is required in your coursework.

Study the following example of a bibliography that lists the four works used in the preceding examples. The first, third, and fourth entries are books. The second entry is a chapter in an edited volume.

Bibliography

Carter, R., and M. McCarthy. 1988. *Vocabulary and language teaching.* New York: Longman.

Eskey, D. 1988. Holding in the bottom: An interactive approach to the language problems of second language readers. In *Interactive approaches to second language reading,* edited by P. Carrell, J. Deveine, and D. Eskey. Cambridge: Cambridge University Press.

Folse, K. 2004. *Vocabulary myths: Applying second language research to classroom teaching.* Ann Arbor: University of Michigan Press.

Wilkins, D. 1972. *Linguistics in language teaching.* London: Edward Arnold.

Appendices

Appendix 1

 Building Better Sentences

Being a good writer involves many skills, such as being able to use correct grammar, vary vocabulary usage, and state ideas concisely. Some student writers like to keep their sentences simple because they feel that if they create longer and more complicated sentences, they are more likely to make mistakes. However, writing short, choppy sentences one after the other is not considered appropriate in academic writing. Study these examples:

The time was yesterday.

It was afternoon.

There was a storm.

The storm was strong.

The movement of the storm was quick.

The storm moved towards the coast.

The coast was in North Carolina.

Notice that every sentence has an important piece of information. A good writer would not write all these sentences separately. Instead, the most important information from each sentence can be used to create one longer, coherent sentence.

Read the sentences again below and notice that the important information has been circled.

The time was yesterday.

It was afternoon.

There was a storm.

The storm was strong.

The movement of the storm was quick.

The storm moved towards the coast.

The coast was in North Carolina.

Here are some strategies for taking the circled information and creating a new sentence.

1. Create time phrases to introduce or end a sentence: *yesterday + afternoon*

2. Find the key noun: *storm*

3. Find key adjectives: *strong*

4. Create noun phrases: *a strong + storm*

5. Change word forms: *movement = move; quick = quickly*

    moved + quickly

6. Create prepositional phrases: *towards the coast*

    towards the coast (of North Carolina)

    or

    towards the North Carolina coast

Now read this improved, longer sentence:

    Yesterday afternoon, a strong storm moved quickly towards the North Carolina coast.

Here are some more strategies for building better sentences:

7. Use coordinating conjunctions (*and, but, or, nor, yet, for, so*) to connect two sets of ideas.

8. Use subordinating conjunctions, such as *after, while, since,* and *because,* to connect related ideas.

9. Use clauses with relative pronouns, such as *who, which, that,* and *whose,* to describe or define a noun or noun phrase.

10. Use pronouns to refer to previously mentioned information.

11. Use possessive adjectives and pronouns, such as *my, her, his, ours,* and *theirs.*

Study the following example.

(Susan) (went) somewhere. That place was (the mall.) Susan wanted to (buy new shoes.) The shoes were for (Susan's mother.)

Now read the improved, longer sentence:

Susan went to the mall because she wanted to buy new shoes for her mother.

Practices

This section contains practices for the sample essays in Units 1–6. Follow these steps for each practice:

1. Read the sentences. Circle the most important information in each sentence.

2. Write an original sentence from the information you circled. Use the strategies listed above.

3. Go back to the original paragraph in the essay to check your sentence. Find the sentence in the paragraph. Compare your sentence with the original sentence. Your goal is not to reproduce the exact original sentence. Your goal is to come up with a sentence that has the same meaning as the original sentence and is expressed in a grammatically correct manner.

Practice 1 Unit 1, "Against E-Voting," page 2

A. (Paragraph 1)

1. For the most part, these innovations promise to save us time.

2. These innovations are technological.

3. They also save money.

4. They also promise to make our lives easier.

5. They also promise to make our lives more comfortable.

_____

_____

B. (Paragraph 2)

1. This process may be tedious.

2. It has a benefit.

3. The benefit is that it is verifiable.

_____

_____

C. (Paragraph 4)

    1. Furthermore, these receipts could be counted by hand.

    2. Furthermore, these receipts could be checked.

    3. These receipts could be checked against the results.

    4. The computers provided the results.

    5. These receipts could be counted if any candidate suspected that the election was unfair.

_____

_____

Practice 2 Unit 2, "Getting the Best Deal" (Essay 2C), page 36

A. (Paragraph 1)

    1. The buyer wants to purchase a product.

    2. The purchase should be at the lowest possible price.

    3. The seller wants to maximize the potential for profit.

_____

_____

B. (Paragraph 3)

    1. If you go back at the end of the day, the sellers will give you discounts.

    2. You go back to buy something.

    3. They will often give discounts.

    4. They give discounts so that they will have fewer products.

    5. They have to pack up these products.

_____

_____

C. (Paragraph 5)

    1. Once you start bargaining, you may find that it becomes a game.

    2. The game is addictive.

    3. In this game, you are competing.

    4. Your competition is the salesperson.

    5. Your goal is your money.

_____

_____

Practice 3 Unit 3, "The Truth about Cats and Dogs" (Essay 3C), page 64

A. (Paragraph 1)

1. He was cold.

2. He was wet.

3. He was hungry.

4. I was afraid of something.

5. The something was that he would die.

6. It might happen on my doorstep.

7. It might happen if I did not help him.

_____

_____

B. (Paragraph 3)

1. We also had another dog.

2. The dog was named Rover.

3. Rover used to bark.

4. The barking was very loud.

5. The barking happened whenever the postal carrier came to deliver our mail.

_____

_____

C. (Paragraph 4)

1. My friend had a cat.

2. My friend's name was Aimee.

3. Her cat was aloof.

4. Her cat was distant.

5. I never saw it when I came to visit.

_____

_____

Practice 4 Unit 4, "Modern Music Technology: Downloading or Stealing?" (Essay 4C), page 92

A. (Paragraph 1)

1. Albums are not selling as much as they were several years ago.

2. CDs are not selling as much as they were several years ago.

3. This is a trend.

4. It shows no sign of reversing.

_____

_____

B. (Paragraph 3)

    1. For this reason, it makes less sense to give away a part of their profits.

    2. It makes less sense for musicians.

    3. The profits go to a record company.

    4. The profits are for activities.

    5. The musicians can accomplish these activities themselves.

_____

_____

C. (Paragraph 5)

    1. The computer has brought about changes.

    2. These changes were to the recording industry.

    3. These changes were tremendous.

    4. The industry will have to move quickly.

    5. The purpose of this quick movement is to retain the relevance of the recording industry.

    6. This relevance is in today's economy.

_____

_____

Practice 5 Unit 5, "Can Spam!" (Essay 5C), page 118

A. (Paragraph 1)

    1. Now it seems that every time I check my e-mail, I delete a parade of advertisements.

    2. I also delete a parade of other correspondence.

    3. This parade is endless.

    4. This correspondence does not come from businesses.

    5. The businesses are legitimate.

    6. The correspondence does not interest me at all.

_____

_____

B. (Paragraph 3)

    1. This problem is troubling.

    2. This problem is with e-mail.

    3. It is troubling for private individuals.

    4. The problem is even worse for businesses.

    5. The businesses are large.

_____

_____

C. (Paragraph 4)

1. Yes, free speech is a component of the exchange of ideas.

2. Free speech is essential.

3. The ideas are necessary for a democracy.

4. The democracy is flourishing.

_____

_____

Practice 6 Unit 6, "Why I Learned English" (Essay 6C), page 148

A. (Paragraph 1)

1. My roots are intertwined.

2. My roots are from my family.

3. My roots are intertwined with different backgrounds.

4. There are several backgrounds.

5. The backgrounds are ethnic.

6. The backgrounds are cultural.

_____

_____

B. (Paragraph 2)

1. We spoke Spanish in our house.

2. My grandparents spoke only English.

3. They were American.

_____

_____

C. (Paragraph 5)

1. Now my grandparents talk on the phone.

2. Now I talk on the phone.

3. We talk on the phone every week.

4. We do not use a translator.

5. Our relationship is much closer than it ever was before.

_____

_____

Appendix 2
Peer Editing Sheets

Writer: _____ Date: _____

Peer Editor: _____

Essay Title: _____

1. What is the general topic of the essay? _____
   _____

2. How many paragraphs are there? _____

3. Do you think the introduction does a good job of introducing the topic? _____
   Explain your answer briefly. _____
   _____

4. Can you identify the thesis statement? Write it here. _____
   _____
   _____

5. Did you find any examples of *this* or *these* as connectors? Write up to three examples here.
   _____
   _____
   _____

6. If you found any spelling errors, write one of them here. _____
   _____

7. If you found any grammar errors, write one of them here. _____
   _____

8. Do you agree with the writer's ideas about this topic? _____ Why or why not? Give examples of

things you agree or disagree with. _____

_____

_____

_____

_____

Peer Editing Sheet 2 Unit 2, Activity 19, page 52
Process Analysis Essay, Step 5

Writer: _____ Date: _____

Peer Editor: _____

Essay Title: _____

1. What process does this essay describe? _____

   _____

2. How many paragraphs are there? _____

3. How many body paragraphs are there? _____ Does each body paragraph have a good topic

   sentence? _____ If you can suggest improvements for one of the topic sentences, write your

   suggestion here. _____

   _____

   _____

4. How is the essay organized? (Circle one.)   **chronologically**   **by priority**

5. Are the steps of the process in logical order? _____ If not, explain your answer here.

   _____

   _____

   _____

6. Were any steps left out that you think should be included? _____ If so, write that step here and

   put a star (*) in the essay to show where the step should be inserted.

   _____

   _____

   _____

7. Did the writer use any time words as transitions? If so, circle them in the essay. If not, mark any places where time words would be helpful.

8. If you found any spelling errors, write one of them here. _____

9. Look for grammar errors, especially those relating to Grammar Topics 2.1–2.5 in this unit. If you found any grammar errors, write one of them here. _____

_____

10. Can you find two words or phrases that make the essay sound advanced? If not, can you suggest two such vocabulary words or phrases and tell the writer where they should be placed in the essay?

_____

_____

Peer Editing Sheet 3 Unit 3, Activity 19, page 80
Comparison Essay, Step 5

Writer: _____ Date: _____

Peer Editor: _____

Essay Title: _____

1. In a few words, what is the essay about? _____

   _____

2. How many paragraphs are there? _____

3. Which method of organization is used? (Circle one.)   **block   point-by-point**

4. Does the writer believe that there are more similarities or more differences between the two subjects?

   _____

5. Can you identify the thesis statement? Write it here. _____

   _____

   _____

6. Comparison essays often use transitions such as *like, similar to, whereas,* and *unlike.* Write two or three examples of comparison transitions that you found in this essay. (If you did not find any, mark places in the essay where transitions would be helpful.)

   _____

   _____

   _____

7. Are the comparisons supported with sufficient and appropriate details? _____ If not, put a star (*) next to the places that need supporting information.

8. Look for grammar errors, especially those relating to Grammar Topics 3.1–3.5 in this unit. If you found any grammar errors, write one of them here. _____

_____

9. One of the worst and most easily corrected composition errors is the fragment. (See page 184.) Does this essay have any fragments? _____ If so, write *FRAG* next to the fragment in the essay and write a possible correction here. _____

_____

_____

10. Does the writer restate the thesis in the conclusion? _____ If not, make a note of this on the essay draft.

6. Can you find two words or phrases that make the essay sound advanced? If not, can you suggest two such vocabulary words or phrases and tell where they should be placed in the essay?

_____

_____

_____

7. Does the writer restate the thesis in the conclusion? _____ If not, make a note of this on the essay draft.

Peer Editing Sheet 4 Unit 4, Activity 19, page 108
Cause-Effect Essay, Step 5

Writer: _____ Date: _____

Peer Editor: _____

Essay Title: _____

1. What is the general topic of the essay? _____

_____

2. How many paragraphs are there? _____

3. Do you agree with the writer's logic and the information he or she presents in this essay? Explain your answer briefly. _____

_____

_____

_____

4. What kind of organization is used? (Circle one.)   **focus-on-effects   focus-on-causes**

5. Fill in the blanks to illustrate the organization of this essay.

Cause: _____

Effects: _____, _____, _____

OR

Effect: _____

Causes: _____, _____, _____

6. Write three to five examples of transitions and connectors that are used to express a cause-effect relationship. If there are none, suggest one or two places where they could be added.

_____

_____

_____

7. Look for grammar errors, especially those relating to Grammar Topics 4.1–4.5 in this unit. If you found any grammar errors, write one of them here. _____

_____

8. In your opinion, are the three causes or three effects believable to you? Does the writer give sufficient support for each of these? Explain your answer. _____

_____

_____

_____

9. Does the writer restate the thesis in the conclusion? _____ If not, make a note of this on the essay draft.

Peer Editing Sheet 5 Unit 5, Activity 20, page 137
Argumentative Essay, Step 5

Writer: _____ Date: _____

Peer Editor: _____

Essay Title: _____

1. In your own words, what is the main point of this essay? (In other words, what is the writer's position on the issue?) _____

_____

_____

2. Examine the writer's supporting evidence. What do you think is the writer's most convincing point in the essay? _____

_____

_____

3. Which of the writer's points is the least convincing? How could this point be improved?

_____

_____

_____

4. Has this essay changed your opinion about this issue? Why or why not?

_____

_____

_____

5. Look for grammar errors, especially those relating to Grammar Topics 5.1–5.5 in this unit. If you found any grammar errors, write one of them here. _____

_____

_____

6. Can you find two words or phrases that make the essay sound advanced? If not, can you suggest two such vocabulary words or phrases and tell where they should be placed in the essay?

_____

_____

_____

7. Does the writer restate the thesis in the conclusion? _____ If not, make a note of this on the essay draft.

Writer: _____ Date: _____

Peer Editor: _____

Essay Title: _____

1. In your own words, what is the main point of this essay? (In other words, what is the writer's position on the issue?) _____

   _____

   _____

2. Examine the writer's supporting evidence. What do you think is the writer's most convincing point in the essay? _____

   _____

   _____

3. Which of the writer's points is the least convincing? How could this point be improved?

   _____

   _____

   _____

4. Has this essay changed your opinion about this issue? Why or why not?

   _____

   _____

   _____

5. Look for grammar errors, especially those relating to Grammar Topics 5.1–5.5 in this unit. If you found any grammar errors, write one of them here. _____

   _____

   _____

6. Write three to five examples of transitions and connectors that are used to express a cause-effect relationship. If there are none, suggest one or two places where they could be added.

_____

_____

_____

7. Look for grammar errors, especially those relating to Grammar Topics 4.1–4.5 in this unit. If you found any grammar errors, write one of them here. _____

_____

8. In your opinion, are the three causes or three effects believable to you? Does the writer give sufficient support for each of these? Explain your answer. _____

_____

_____

_____

9. Does the writer restate the thesis in the conclusion? _____ If not, make a note of this on the essay draft.

Peer Editing Sheet 4 Unit 4, Activity 19, page 108
Cause-Effect Essay, Step 5

Writer: _____ Date: _____

Peer Editor: _____

Essay Title: _____

1. What is the general topic of the essay? _____

   _____

2. How many paragraphs are there? _____

3. Do you agree with the writer's logic and the information he or she presents in this essay? Explain your

   answer briefly. _____

   _____

   _____

   _____

4. What kind of organization is used? (Circle one.)   **focus-on-effects   focus-on-causes**

5. Fill in the blanks to illustrate the organization of this essay.

   Cause: _____

   Effects: _____, _____, _____

OR

   Effect: _____

   Causes: _____, _____, _____